SOUPS & BROTHS

10 9 8 7 6 5 4 3 2 1

BBC Books, an imprint of Ebury Publishing
20 Vauxhall Bridge Road,
London SW1V 2SA

BBC Books is part of the Penguin Random House group of companies whose addresses can be found at
global.penguinrandomhouse.com

Penguin
Random House
UK

Photographs © BBC Magazines 2016
Recipes © BBC Worldwide 2016
Book design © Woodlands Books Ltd 2016
All recipes contained in this book first appeared in BBC *Good Food* magazine.

First published by BBC Books in 2016

www.eburypublishing.co.uk

ISBN 9781785941948

Printed and bound in China by Toppan Leefung

Project editor: Charlotte Macdonald
Design: Interstate Creative Partners Ltd and Kathryn Gammon
Cover Design: Interstate Creative Partners Ltd
Production: Alex Goddard
Picture Researcher: Gabby Harrington

PICTURE AND RECIPE CREDITS

BBC Books would like to thank the following people for providing photos. While every effort has been made to trace and
acknowledge all photographers, we should like to apologise should there be any errors or omissions.

Will Heap 11, 19, 65, 123, 135, 137; Mike English 13, 53, 71, 79, 97, 189; Myles New 15, 47, 55, 127, 147, 149, 163, 175; Lis Parsons 17,
69, 73, 93, 105, 161, 165, 197; Kate Whitaker 23; David Munns 29, 41, 43, 83, 101, 107, 113, 119, 141, 153, 159, 173, 185, 187, 193
Stuart Ovenden 27, 31, 67, 81, 201 Roger Stowell 33 Rob Streeter 35, 89, 95, 103, 171, 209 Tim Winter 37 Simon Brown 39; Sam
Stowell 45, 143, 155, 167, 179; Ken Field 49 Philip Webb 51, 75, 99, 145, 199; Gareth Morgans 57, 111, 117, 139, 157, 177, 191, 195
Debi Treloar 59 Craig Robertson 61 Jean Cazals 63, 77, 205; Maja Smend 85; Toby Scott 87; Simon Smith 91; Adrian Lawrence 109,
115, 131; Yuki Sugiura 121; Dawie Verwey 125; Peter Williams 129; Howard Shooter 133; Carolyn Barber 169; Jason Lowe 181;
William Lingwood 183; Peter Cassidy 203.

All the recipes in this book were created by the editorial team at *Good Food* and by regular contributors to BBC Magazines.

SOUPS & BROTHS

Editor **Chelsie Collins**

BOOKS

Contents

Introduction

Soups come in many varieties: smooth and velvety, chunky and creamy or clear and packed with flavour. Whether a starter for entertaining friends, a quick mid-week meal, light lunch or to soothe a cold and warm you up, a soup can start a meal perfectly or even be a meal in itself.

This is *BBC Good Food*'s collection of healthier soup and broth recipes – some of these are low in fat, some low in calories (see chapter 4), but one thing is for sure, they are all healthy and packed full of nutrients.

At *Good Food* eating well is everything. We pride ourselves on providing delicious, balanced recipes, which inspire you to cook more creatively. I hope this collection of recipes does just that. Our feel good broths and nourishing chapters are perfect if you are feeling under the weather and looking for a bowl of goodness, while our hearty soups with pulses and grains will make you feel fuller for longer. Low calorie and summer soups and broths are a little lighter, for when the weather gets warmer. Whatever the occasion, we hope this book is well used in your kitchen, and as always, every recipe has been triple tested by the *BBC Good Food* cookery team, so will work every time.

Chelsie C.

Chelsie Collins, Cookery Writer
BBC Good Food magazine

Notes & conversion tables

. . . .

NOTES ON THE RECIPES
- Eggs are large in the UK and Australia and extra large in America unless stated.
- Wash fresh produce before preparation.
- Recipes contain nutritional analyses for 'sugars', which means the total sugar content including all natural sugars in the ingredients, unless otherwise stated.

OVEN TEMPERATURES

GAS	°C	°C FAN	°F	OVEN TEMP.
¼	110	90	225	Very cool
½	120	100	250	Very cool
1	140	120	275	Cool or slow
2	150	130	300	Cool or slow
3	160	140	325	Warm
4	180	160	350	Moderate
5	190	170	375	Moderately hot
6	200	180	400	Fairly hot
7	220	200	425	Hot
8	230	210	450	Very hot
9	240	220	475	Very hot

APPROXIMATE WEIGHT CONVERSIONS
- All the recipes in this book list both metric and imperial measurements. Conversions are approximate and have been rounded up or down. Follow one set of measurements only; do not mix the two.
- Cup measurements, which are used in Australia and America, have not been listed here as they vary from ingredient to ingredient. Kitchen scales should be used to measure dry/solid ingredients.

Good Food is concerned about sustainable sourcing and animal welfare. Where possible, humanely reared meats, sustainably caught fish (see fishonline.org for further information from the Marine Conservation Society) and free-range chickens and eggs are used when recipes are originally tested.

SPOON MEASURES

Spoon measurements are level unless otherwise specified.

- 1 teaspoon (tsp) = 5ml
- 1 tablespoon (tbsp) = 15ml
- 1 Australian tablespoon = 20ml (cooks in Australia should measure 3 teaspoons where 1 tablespoon is specified in a recipe)

APPROXIMATE LIQUID CONVERSIONS

METRIC	IMPERIAL	AUS	US
50ml	2fl oz	¼ cup	¼ cup
125ml	4fl oz	½ cup	½ cup
175ml	6fl oz	¾ cup	¾ cup
225ml	8fl oz	1 cup	1 cup
300ml	10fl oz/½ pint	½ pint	1¼ cups
450ml	16fl oz	2 cups	2 cups/1 pint
600ml	20fl oz/1 pint	1 pint	2½ cups
1 litre	35fl oz/1¾ pints	1¾ pints	1 quart

Chicken noodle soup

· ·

Feeling under the weather? This soup will sort you out in no time. Ginger is particularly good for colds, and the aromatic broth will help you feel soothed and comforted.

🕐 PREP 10 mins COOK 30 mins   2

- 900ml/1½ pints chicken or vegetable stock (or Miso soup mix)
- 1 skinless chicken breast, about 175g/6oz
- 1 tsp chopped ginger
- 1 garlic clove, finely chopped
- 50g/2oz rice or wheat noodles
- 2 tbsp sweetcorn, canned or frozen
- 2-3 mushrooms, thinly sliced
- 2 spring onions, shredded
- 2 tsp soy sauce, plus extra for serving
- mint or basil leaves and a little shredded chilli (optional), to serve
- lime wedges, to serve

1 Pour the stock into a pan and add the chicken, ginger and garlic. Bring to the boil, then reduce the heat, partly cover and simmer for 20 mins, until the chicken is tender. Remove the chicken to a board and shred into bite-sized pieces using a couple of forks.
2 Return the chicken to the stock with the noodles, corn, mushrooms, half the spring onions and the soy sauce. Simmer for 3-4 mins until the noodles are tender. Ladle into two bowls and scatter over the remaining spring onions, herbs and chilli shreds, if using. Serve with extra soy sauce for sprinkling over and lime wedges.

MAKE IT VEGGIE Replace the chicken breast with 175g/6oz firm tofu cut into cubes, simmer for about 5 mins, then add the other ingredients as before.

· ·
PER SERVING 217 kcals, fat 2g, saturates 0.4g, carbs 26g, sugars 1g, fibre 0.6g, protein 26g, salt 2.52g

Bone broth

. . . .

Cooking chicken carcasses for a longer period of time helps to extract the minerals from the bones, making the broth more nourishing.

🕐 PREP 20 mins COOK 45 mins   4

- 1 meaty chicken carcass, plus any jellified roasting juices from it, skin and fat discarded
- 1 large onion, halved and sliced
- zest and juice 1 lemon
- 2 bay leaves
- 1-2 red chillies, halved, deseeded and sliced
- 1 tsp ground coriander
- ½ tsp ground cumin
- small pack coriander, stems and leaves chopped and separated
- 1 large garlic clove, finely grated

SUPERCHARGED TOPPING
- 250g pouch wholegrain basmati rice

1 Break the chicken carcass into a large pan and add the onion, 1.5 litres/2¾ pints of water, the lemon juice and bay leaves. Cover and simmer for 40 mins. Remove from the heat and allow to cool slightly, to make things a bit easier to handle.

2 Place a colander over a bowl and scoop out all the bones into the colander. Pick through them, stripping off the chicken and returning it with any onion as you work your way down the pile of bones.

3 Return any broth from the bowl to the pan – and any jellified roasting juices – along with the chilli, ground coriander, cumin, coriander stems, lemon zest and garlic. Cook for a few mins until just bubbling – don't overboil as you will spoil the delicate flavours. Taste, and season only if you need to. Meanwhile, heat the rice following pack instructions, then toss with the coriander leaves. Ladle the broth into bowls and top with the rice.

. . . .
PER SERVING 150 kcals, fat 3g, saturates 1g, carbs 24g, sugars 5g, fibre 2g, protein 6g, salt 0.9g

Spicy prawn soup

This soup will be on the table in 15 mins. If you can't find coconut milk, feel free to substitute for coconut cream, diluted as instructed.

🕐 PREP 5 mins COOK 15 mins   4

- 1 tbsp sunflower oil
- 300g bag crunchy stir-fry vegetables
- 140g/5oz shiitake mushrooms, sliced
- 2 tbsp Thai green curry paste
- 400g can reduced-fat coconut milk
- 200ml/7fl oz vegetable or fish stock
- 300g/10oz medium straight-to-wok noodles
- 200g bag large, raw prawns

1 Heat a wok, add the oil, then stir-fry the veg and mushrooms for 2-3 mins. Take out and set aside, then tip the curry paste into the pan and fry for 1 min. Pour in the coconut milk and stock. Bring to the boil, drop in the noodles and prawns, then reduce the heat and simmer for 4 mins until the prawns are cooked through. Stir in the veg, then serve.

PER SERVING 327 kcals, fat 17g, saturates 10g, carbs 32g, sugars 4g, fibre 4g, protein 16g, salt 0.97g

Salmon noodle soup

This heart healthy, good source of omega-3 noodle soup is low fat and counts as 1 of your 5-a-day.

PREP 15 mins COOK 20 mins 4

- 1 litre/1¾ pints low-sodium chicken stock
- 2 tsp Thai red curry paste
- 100g/4oz flat rice noodles
- 150g pack shiitake mushrooms, sliced
- 125g pack baby corn, sliced
- 2 skinless salmon fillets, sliced
- juice 2 limes
- 1 tbsp low-salt soy sauce
- pinch brown sugar
- small bunch coriander, chopped

1 Pour the stock into a large pan, bring to the boil, then stir in the curry paste. Add the noodles and cook for 8 mins. Tip in the mushrooms and baby corn and cook for 2 mins more.

2 Add the salmon to the pan and cook for 3 mins or until cooked through. Remove from the heat and stir in the lime juice, soy sauce and a pinch of sugar. Ladle into 4 bowls and sprinkle over the chopped coriander just before you serve.

PER SERVING 265 kcals, fat 10g, saturates 2g, carbs 27g, sugars 4g, fibre 1g, protein 19g, salt 0.83g

Turkey noodle soup

· ·

Use up chicken or turkey in this broth, and spice it up with sliced red chillies if you like a bit of a kick.

 PREP 10 mins COOK 10 mins   4

- 1.2 litres/2 pints low-sodium chicken stock
- 4 small carrots, peeled and chopped
- 140g/5oz medium egg noodles
- 200g/7oz shredded, cooked turkey or chicken
- 200g/7oz frozen peas
- 1 bunch spring onions, sliced, white and green parts separated

1 Bring the stock to the boil and throw in the carrots. Boil for 4 mins, then add the noodles and simmer for 3 mins. Stir in the turkey, peas and the white part of the spring onions, heat for 1 min or until everything is hot through. Ladle into bowls, scatter with the green part of the onions and serve.

· ·

PER SERVING 285 kcals, fat 6g, saturates 1g, carbs 36g, sugars 6g, fibre 5g, protein 23g, salt 0.42g

Quick & easy hot-&-sour chicken noodle soup

When seasoning the broth, enhance the 'hot and sour' flavour with as much chilli and rice vinegar as you like.

 PREP 25 mins COOK 15 mins 2

- 140g/5oz dried wholewheat noodles
- 1 tbsp groundnut oil
- 2 tbsp grated ginger
- 1 medium red chilli, deseeded and finely chopped
- 4 boneless, skinless chicken thighs, chopped into small chunks
- 1 tbsp Shaohsing rice wine
- 700ml/1¼ pints hot vegetable stock
- 4 chestnut mushrooms, sliced
- 1 tsp dark soy sauce
- 2 tbsp light soy sauce
- 2 tbsp rice vinegar
- 1 tbsp cornflour mixed with 2 tbsp cold water to make a paste
- 1 handful beansprouts
- 2 spring onions, sliced

1 Bring a small pan of water to the boil and cook the noodles following pack instructions. Drain, rinse under cold running water to stop them cooking further, then drizzle over a little oil to prevent them sticking together. Divide between 2 deep bowls.

2 Heat a wok over high heat and add the rest of the oil. When it starts to smoke, add the ginger and chilli, then stir-fry for a few secs. Add the chicken and stir-fry for 2 mins. As the meat starts to turn brown, add the rice wine and cook for 3 mins more. Add the vegetable stock, bring to a simmer, then add the mushrooms. Season with the dark soy, light soy and rice vinegar. Bring back to a simmer, then add the cornflour paste. Simmer and stir until thickened. Stir in the beansprouts and most of the spring onions, then ladle the soup over the noodles. Serve immediately, scattered with the remaining spring onions.

PER SERVING 407 kcals, fat 12g, saturates 3g, carbs 33g, sugars 6g, fibre 5g, protein 42g, salt 5.1g

Kale & chorizo broth

Kale is rich in immune supporting nutrients such as beta-carotene and vitamin C, which help to maintain healthy skin.

PREP 15 mins COOK 30 mins 6

- 3 tbsp olive oil
- 2 onions, finely chopped
- 4 garlic cloves, crushed
- 2-3 cooking chorizo sausages, sliced
- 4 large potatoes
- 1.5 litres/2¾ pints chicken stock
- 200g/7oz curly kale, finely shredded

1 Heat 2 tbsp of the oil in a large saucepan. Add the onion, garlic and chorizo, then cook for 5 mins until soft. Throw in the potatoes and cook for a few mins more. Pour in the stock, season and bring to the boil. Cook everything for 10 mins until the potatoes are on the brink of collapse.

2 Use a masher to squash the potatoes into the soup, then bring back to the boil. Add the kale and cook for 5 mins until tender. Ladle the soup into bowls, then serve drizzled with the remaining olive oil.

PER SERVING 314 kcals, fat 14g, saturates 3g, carbs 30g, sugars 5g, fibre 4g, protein 19g, salt 1.7g

Curried vegetable broth

A classic vegetable broth with a spicy twist.

PREP 20 mins COOK 30 mins 4

- 1 tbsp olive oil
- 1 medium onion, finely chopped
- 2 medium celery sticks, chopped
- 1 large potato, chopped
- 2 carrots, chopped,
- 1 parsnip, chopped into large chunks
- 2 tbsp mild vegetarian curry paste
- 1 tbsp plain flour
- 850ml/1½ pints vegetable stock
- 2 tbsp double cream

FOR THE GARNISH
- 15g butter
- 1 large onion, finely sliced
- 2 tbsp chopped coriander

1 Heat the oil in a large pan, then add the vegetables. Toss well and cook for 3-4 mins until lightly browned.
2 Stir in curry paste and flour and mix together well. Pour over the stock and bring to the boil. Leave to simmer for 20-30 mins until the vegetables are tender.
3 Meanwhile, for the garnish, heat the butter in a frying pan and gently cook the onion for 7-10 mins until browned.
4 Stir the cream into the soup. Serve immediately sprinkled with the fried onion and chopped coriander.

PER SERVING 209 kcals, fat 14g, saturates 5g, carbs 18g, sugars 0g, fibre 4g, protein 4g, salt 0.92g

Jogaetang – Korean clam broth

This broth is perfect if you want to cook something simple and special, but you're short on time. It's very low calorie too.

PREP 10 mins COOK 10 mins 4

- 500g/1lb 2 oz medium-sized clams, rinsed
- 1 tbsp gochujang chilli paste or white miso if you don't want it to be spicy
- 2 large garlic cloves, finely chopped
- 3 spring onions, finely sliced, white and green parts separated
- 2 handfuls beansprouts
- 1 green chilli, cut into matchsticks
- toasted sesame oil, to serve
- cooked rice and kimchi or pickled cucumber, to serve

1 Drain the rinsed clams well and place them in a saucepan (with a lid) that fits them in a single layer. Pour over cold water to just cover (about 750ml/1⅓ pints should do it), then stir in the chilli paste, the garlic and the spring onion whites.

2 Cover with a lid, bring to the boil, then turn down the heat and simmer gently for 2-3 mins until the clams have all opened. Turn off the heat and stir through the beansprouts and chilli. Season with salt to taste, and decant into 1 large or 2 smaller bowls. Top with the spring onion greens and a drizzle of sesame oil, and enjoy with rice and something sharp like kimchi or pickled cucumber. You'll need soup spoons and a bowl for the empty shells.

PER SERVING 61 kcals, fat 1g, saturates 0g, carbs 3g, sugars 1g, fibre 1g, protein 9g, salt 1.0g

Mussels in spiced broth

This delicious seafood broth can take a lot of spice because of the natural sweetness from the coconut.

🕐 PREP 20 mins COOK 10 mins   2

- 5 coriander sprigs, leaves and stems separated, plus extra for serving
- 400ml can coconut milk
- 2 lemongrass stalks, halved and bruised
- thumb-size piece ginger, thickly sliced (or galangal if you have it)
- 6 lime leaves, crushed
- 2 small green chillies, crushed
- 125ml/4fl oz coconut cream
- 500g/1lb 2oz mussels, scrubbed
- 2 tbsp fish sauce
- 2 tbsp lime juice

1 Crush the coriander stems in a mortar using a pestle, then put into a large pan with the coconut milk, lemongrass and ginger. Bring to the boil and simmer for 4 mins. Add the lime leaves and the chillies, then stir in the coconut cream.

2 Add the mussels and fish sauce, then cover with an ill-fitting lid or baking tray so that the mussels can steam, but the broth won't boil over and make a mess of your stove. Bring the liquid back to the boil, then simmer for a few mins, shaking the pot every so often so the mussels move around and open up – this should take about 3-5 mins.

3 When all the mussels are open, add the lime juice but don't boil again. Taste, and if you like it, good – otherwise add more chilli for heat, more lime for sourness and more fish sauce if you think it needs salt. Spoon into bowls and sprinkle with the coriander leaves to serve.

PER SERVING 623 kcals, fat 55g, saturates 47g, carbs 14g, sugars 10g, fibre 0g, protein 17g, salt 4.07g

Ramen with pork, soft egg & greens

You can get as complicated as you like with homemade ramen broth, but this version will give you a fabulous depth of flavour without having to find unusual ingredients.

 PREP 25 mins COOK 4 hrs 10 mins 4

- 4 eggs
- 250g/9oz ramen noodles
- 2 large handfuls shredded spring greens
- 4 spring onions, finely chopped
- 75g/2½oz bamboo shoots from a can, drained, chopped and soaked in 2 tbsp rice vinegar
- chilli oil and pickled chilli & shallots, to serve

FOR THE RAMEN STOCK
- 6 chicken legs
- 2 large carrots, halved
- 2 onions, quartered
- 4cm/1½in piece ginger, sliced
- 900g/2lb pork shoulder (thick layer of fat removed), halved
- 4 dried shiitake mushrooms

FOR THE RAMEN SEASONING
- 1 tbsp mirin
- 1 tbsp sake
- 4 tbsp Japanese soy sauce

1 Heat oven to 200C/180C fan/gas 6. Put the chicken, carrot, onion and ginger in a large roasting tin. Season and roast for 30 mins, then transfer to a large pan. Add the pork, mushroom and 3 litres/5 pints water. Bring to the boil, then gently simmer for 3 hours. Skim foam that rises to the top and partly cover with a lid. Remove the pork after 2½ hours, or when very soft. Strain the stock into a pan (use the chicken for something else). Boil for 30-40 mins on medium heat to reduce by a third, then skim any fat. Add 1 tsp salt to taste.

2 Boil the eggs for 6 mins, then remove and put in iced water to cool. Peel and halve. Boil the noodles, stirring so they don't stick, for 3 mins until al dente. In the final minute, add the greens. Drain and divide among the bowls.

3 Mix the ramen seasoning ingredients. Slice the pork and add to the bowls. Pour the broth over and add the spring onion, bamboo and eggs with the chilli & shallots. Serve with the chilli oil and ramen seasoning on the side.

PER SERVING 798 kcals, fat 32g, saturates 10g, carbs 51g, sugars 4g, fibre 4g, protein 71g, salt 6.0g

Hot-&-sour coconut soup

. . . .

A really light, subtle soup with plenty of fresh vibrant flavours. Adding the rice makes it more substantial for a main meal, or serve it without for a starter.

⏱ PREP 15 mins COOK 25-30 mins   🍽 4

- 100g/4oz Thai fragrant rice
- 1.2 litres/2 pints chicken or vegetable stock
- 1 lemongrass stalk, thinly sliced
- 1 tbsp finely chopped galangal or ginger
- 4 fresh or freeze-dried lime leaves, chopped or crumbled
- 2 red chillies, deseeded and finely chopped
- 250g/9oz skinless chicken breast, thinly sliced
- 175g/6oz chestnut mushrooms, sliced
- 200g/7oz cherry tomatoes, halved
- 1 tbsp lime juice
- 2 tbsp fish sauce (nam pla)
- 200ml carton coconut cream
- handful coriander, chopped

1 Cook the rice in boiling salted water for about 10 minutes, until tender, then drain well and set aside.
2 Meanwhile, heat the stock in a large pan, add the lemongrass, galangal or ginger, lime leaves and chillies and simmer for 5 minutes. Add the chicken and mushrooms and simmer for a further 5 minutes. Stir in the tomatoes, lime juice, fish sauce and coconut cream and simmer for 5 minutes more. Scatter over the coriander and serve each portion with a little cooked rice spooned in.

. . . .

PER SERVING 356 kcals, fat 19g, saturates 15g, carbs 26g, sugars 0g, fibre 1g, protein 22g, salt 2.47g

Oyster beef with soupy noodles

No need for a Chinese takeaway when you can make it yourself with half the fat and calorie content, and twice the flavour!

PREP 15 mins COOK 10 mins   4

- 3 nests (about 200g/7oz) medium egg noodles
- 1 litre/1¾ pints beef stock
- thumb-sized piece ginger, cut into matchsticks
- bunch spring onions, white parts sliced thickly at an angle, green chopped
- 1 tsp Chinese five-spice powder
- 1 red chilli, deseeded and sliced
- 2 tbsp soy sauce
- 1 tbsp sesame oil
- 2 sirloin steaks (about 400g/14oz), trimmed of fat and thinly sliced across the grain
- 2-3 tbsp oyster sauce

1 Put a kettle of water on to boil and the noodles in a bowl. Tip the stock, ginger, whites of the onions and the five-spice into a large pan and leave to simmer for 5 mins.

2 When the kettle boils, pour the water over the noodles and leave to soak for 3 mins (they should be softened, but not completely), then drain. Now add to the stock pan with the chilli, spring onion greens, soy sauce and half the sesame oil, and cook about 2 mins more.

3 Meanwhile, heat the remaining oil in a large wok. Add the beef and stir-fry over a high heat for about 1 min until it changes colour, but is still a little rare in the centre. Spoon in the oyster sauce and cook over the heat to coat the beef. Ladle the noodles and liquid into bowls and top with the oyster beef.

PER SERVING 391 kcals, fat 11g, saturates 3g, carbs 36g, sugars 2g, fibre 3g, protein 34g, salt 2.7g

Essence of tomatoes

. . . .

This soup can be made a day ahead and left in the fridge overnight. It makes an impressive starter when you are entertaining guests.

PREP 40-50 mins plus marinating and cooling NO COOK 4

- 2.5kg/5½lb vine-ripened cherry tomatoes, roughly chopped
- 1 celery stick, finely chopped
- 1 small shallot, finely chopped
- ½ fennel bulb, finely chopped
- 1 garlic clove, finely chopped
- 2 sprigs thyme, roughly chopped
- 4 leaves tarragon, roughly chopped
- handful basil leaves, roughly chopped
- 1 tbsp golden caster sugar
- 2 pinches cayenne pepper
- 5 drops Worcestershire sauce
- 3 drops Tabasco

TO SERVE
- 6 large vine plum tomatoes, skinned, deseeded and diced
- 4 basil leaves, finely sliced, plus 4 small sprigs
- good-quality extra virgin olive oil

1 In a large bowl mix all the ingredients together with 1 tbsp sea salt, cover with cling film and marinate for 6 hrs. Then, in a food processor, pulse the tomato mix in batches until roughly chopped – don't over-chop them to a mush.

2 Place 3 layers of muslin cloth, or a new kitchen cloth, over a large bowl and pour the mix into the cloth. Tie up with string and hang in a cold place for at least 15 mins over the bowl to collect the tomato essence. Discard the pulp. Taste and correct the seasoning, if necessary, then cool in the fridge.

3 To serve, spoon a quarter of the diced tomato into the centre of 4 bowls. Carefully pour the chilled tomato essence around the tomato towers and garnish with the basil and a small drizzling of olive oil.

. . . .
PER SERVING 141 kcals, fat 3g, saturates 0g, carbs 25g, sugars 4g, fibre 7g, protein 6g, salt 0.30g

Spring greens & gammon soup

This rustic broth is deliciously meaty and works with gammon or leftover ham.

PREP 10 mins COOK 2 hrs 4

- 450g/1lb piece gammon, soaked overnight
- 2 bay leaves
- 2 medium onions, sliced
- 2 tsp paprika
- 2 large potatoes, peeled and chopped into small chunks
- 225g/8oz spring greens, roughly chopped
- 450g can cannellini beans, drained and washed

1 Put the gammon in a large pan with the bay leaves, onion and about 1.5 litres/2¾ pints of cold water or enough to cover. Bring to the boil, then reduce the heat and simmer gently for about 1½ hours.

2 Drain the gammon, reserving the cooking liquid. When the gammon is cool enough to handle, trim away the skin, and shred the meat.

3 Return the meat to the pan with the reserved cooking liquid, paprika and potatoes. Cover and simmer for 20 mins or until the potatoes are cooked.

4 While the potatoes are cooking, trim away the stalky bit from the greens and finely shred the leaf. Stir the greens and beans into the stock and continue to cook for about 10 mins.

PER SERVING 350 kcals, fat 12g, saturates 4g, carbs 32g, sugars 4g, fibre 7g, protein 30g, salt 3.33g

Chicken, sweetcorn & noodle soup

This low-fat soup is so easy to prepare and is packed full of flavour.

PREP 15 mins COOK 1½ hrs 8

- 2 large carrots, chopped
- 2 large leeks, trimmed and finely sliced
- 2 corn on the cobs, corn kernels cut off
- 200g/7oz vermicelli noodles
- small bunch parsley, finely chopped

FOR THE STOCK

- 2 onions, quartered
- 1 leek, cut into chunks
- 2 carrots, thickly sliced
- 2 bay leaves
- 6 black peppercorns
- parsley stalks
- 4 celery sticks, roughly chopped
- 2 tbsp vegetable bouillon or 1 vegetable stock cube
- 1.3kg/3lb chicken

1 Put all the stock ingredients and the chicken in a very large saucepan, cover everything with about 3 litres/5 pints cold water. Bring to the boil, then lower to a simmer and cook for 1 hr-1½ hrs, until the chicken is cooked through. Skim off any froth every 20 mins or so. Remove the chicken to a plate to cool. Strain the stock through a sieve, skimming off as much fat as you can.

2 Rinse out the pan and put the stock back in, then simmer on a high heat until reduced a little – you need about 2 litres/3½ pints. Add the carrot and leek, then simmer for 10 mins.

3 Meanwhile, shred the meat from the chicken, discarding the skin and bones. Add to the pan with the corn. Add the noodles, unless you want to freeze the soup, and simmer for about 7 mins more, until the corn and pasta are cooked. Ladle into bowls and sprinkle with parsley. To freeze, allow the soup to cool completely before freezing and when you're ready to eat, let the soup defrost before bringing it back to a gentle simmer in a pan. Add the noodles and simmer until cooked.

PER SERVING 288 kcals, fat 9g, saturates 3g, carbs 28g, sugars 5g, fibre 2g, protein 25g, salt 0.71g

Udon noodle soup

This quick-and-easy soup is the perfect midweek meal. It's low-fat, low-calorie and only takes 10 mins to prepare. If you prefer rice noodles, you can use them instead.

PREP 5 mins COOK 10 mins 4

- 1 vegetable stock cube
- 50ml/2fl oz teriyaki sauce
- 1 tbsp vegetable oil
- 140g/5oz chestnut mushrooms, sliced
- ½ bunch spring onions, thinly sliced
- 140g/5oz udon noodles
- 200g bag spinach

1 In a large pan, dissolve the stock cube in 1 litre/1¾ pints of water and stir in the teriyaki sauce. While the soup base comes to the boil, heat the oil in a frying pan and cook the mushrooms over a high heat, for 2-3 mins, until they turn golden. Add the spring onions and cook for 1 min more, then set aside.

2 Once the soup base has come to the boil, add the noodles and cook for 4 mins. Add the spinach and cook for 1 min more until just wilted. Stir in the mushrooms, spring onions and some seasoning, and serve.

PER SERVING 124 kcals, fat 4g, saturates 0g, carbs 17g, sugars 8g, fibre 3g, protein 5g, salt 1.9g

Poached fish with ginger & sesame broth

Fresh Asian flavours liven up this low-fat, low-calorie poached fish broth. Choose your favourite fresh white fish for a wholesome supper.

PREP 8 mins COOK 10 mins 2

- 500ml/18fl oz weak fish stock
- 1 tbsp rice wine vinegar
- 2 slices ginger
- 2 garlic cloves, shredded
- 85g/3oz frozen soya beans or peas
- 100g/4oz Tenderstem broccoli, halved if large
- 4 Chinese leaves, sliced, or 1 small pak choi
- 3 spring onions, sliced at an angle
- 2 chunky white fish fillets, such as haddock or sustainable cod
- few drops sesame oil
- ½-1 tsp toasted sesame seeds

1 Pour the stock into a deep sauté pan or wok with the vinegar, then add the ginger and garlic. Cover and cook for 5 mins to allow the flavours to mingle.

2 Add the soya beans, broccoli and the fleshy part of the Chinese leaves, then place the spring onions and fish on top. Cover and cook for 4-5 mins more until the fish just flakes. Carefully lift the fish off, discard the ginger, and stir in the remaining Chinese leaf and the sesame oil. Ladle into bowls, top with the fish and sprinkle with the seeds.

PER SERVING 247 kcals, fat 6g, saturates 1g, carbs 6g, sugars 1g, fibre 5g, protein 40g, salt 0.7g

Walkers' wild mushroom, bacon & barley broth

· ·

Dried porcini mushrooms give this low-fat soup its rich flavour, which the barley and veg soak up.

PREP 20 mins COOK 1 hr 15 mins　　6

- 200g pack bacon lardons or rashers bacon, cut into small pieces
- 2 onions, finely chopped
- 4 medium carrots, finely chopped
- 3 celery sticks, finely chopped
- 2 garlic cloves, crushed
- 1 sprig each rosemary and thyme
- 30g pack dried porcini or dried mixed wild mushrooms
- 1 glass white wine
- 1.5 litres/2¾ pints chicken stock
- 175g/6oz pearl barley, well rinsed
- 1 small head spring greens or chunk of Savoy cabbage, finely shredded
- Parmesan or any strong hard cheese, grated, to serve

1 Put a large pan over a medium heat. Sizzle the bacon for 10 mins until golden, stirring now and then. Stir in the veg, garlic and herbs, cover and gently cook for 10 mins.

2 Meanwhile, put the mushrooms into a jug, then fill up to the 600ml/1 pint mark with boiling water. Leave to soak for 10 mins.

3 Lift the mushrooms out of their juice and roughly chop. Turn up the heat under the pan, add the mushrooms, fry for 1 min, then pour in the wine. Let it evaporate, then pour in the liquid from the mushroom jug. Add the stock and barley. Simmer for 40 mins until the barley is tender. Lift out the herb stalks. Can be made up to 2 days ahead or frozen for up to 1 month. If you make ahead, the soup will need loosening with a little more stock as the barley will thicken it over time.

4 When ready to serve, simmer the greens in the soup for 5 mins until tender. Season, then serve with cheese for sprinkling over the top.

· ·

PER SERVING 290 kcals, fat 9g, saturates 3g, carbs 35g, sugars 9g, fibre 5g, protein 18g, salt 1.75g

All-in-one chunky winter broth

This tasty low-fat vegetarian soup will be on the table in 20 mins. Replace spinach with another leafy green like kale if you like.

 PREP 5 mins COOK 15-20 minutes 4

- 2 x 400g cans chopped tomatoes
- 2 litres/3½ pints vegetable stock
- 4 carrots, peeled and sliced
- 2 x 420g cans mixed pulses, drained and rinsed
- 175g/6oz spinach
- 1 tbsp roasted red pepper pesto

1 Tip the canned tomatoes into a saucepan along with the stock, bring to the boil, then turn down the heat and throw in the carrots. Gently simmer the soup until the carrots are cooked, about 15 minutes.
2 Stir in the pulses and spinach and heat until the spinach has wilted. Spoon in the pesto and gently mix into the soup. Serve with some crusty bread.

PER SERVING 219 kcals, fat 3g, saturates 1g, carbs 34g, sugars 0g, fibre 12g, protein 16g, salt 3.61g

Butternut squash soup with chilli & crème fraîche

· ·

This vegetarian soup is warming with just the right amount of heat from the chilli. If you like it really spicy, add a little more chilli.

⏱ PREP 15 mins COOK 45-50 mins   🍴 4

- 1 butternut squash, about 1kg/2lb 4oz, peeled and deseeded
- 2 tbsp olive oil
- 1 tbsp butter
- 2 onions, diced
- 1 garlic clove, thinly sliced
- 2 mild red chillies, deseeded and finely chopped
- 850ml/1½ pints hot vegetable stock
- 4 tbsp crème fraîche, plus more to serve

1 Heat oven to 200C/180C fan/gas 6. Cut the squash into large cubes, about 4cm/1½in across, then toss in a large roasting tin with half the olive oil. Roast for 30 mins, turning once during cooking, until golden and soft.

2 While the squash cooks, melt the butter with the remaining oil in a large saucepan, then add the onion, garlic and three-quarters of the chilli. Cover and cook on a very low heat for 15-20 mins until the onion is completely soft.

3 Tip the squash into the pan, add the stock and the crème fraîche, then whizz with a stick blender until smooth. For a really silky soup, put the soup into a blender and blitz it in batches. Return to the pan, gently reheat, then season to taste. Serve the soup in bowls with swirls of crème fraîche and a scattering of the remaining chopped chilli.

· ·
PER SERVING 264 kcals, fat 15g, saturates 7g, carbs 28g, sugars 17g, fibre 6g, protein 5g, salt 0.61g

Carrot & ginger soup

Carrot and ginger are immune boosting if you are feeling full of cold. This soup is also low fat and 3 of your 5-a-day.

PREP 15 mins COOK 25-30 mins   4

- 1 tbsp rapeseed oil
- 1 large onion, chopped
- 2 tbsp coarsely grated ginger
- 2 garlic cloves, sliced
- ½ tsp ground nutmeg
- 850ml/1½ pints vegetable stock
- 500g/1lb 2oz carrots (preferably organic), sliced
- 400g can cannellini beans (no need to drain)

SUPERCHARGED TOPPING
- 4 tbsp almonds in their skins, cut into slivers
- sprinkle of nutmeg

1 Heat the oil in a large pan, add the onion, ginger and garlic, and fry for 5 mins until starting to soften. Stir in the nutmeg and cook for 1 min more.

2 Pour in the stock, add the carrots, beans and their liquid, then cover and simmer for 20-25 mins until the carrots are tender.

3 Scoop a third of the mixture into a bowl and blitz the remainder with a stick blender or in a food processor until smooth. Return everything to the pan and heat until bubbling. Serve topped with the almonds and nutmeg.

PER SERVING 293 kcals, fat 12g, saturates 1g, carbs 31g, sugars 19g, fibre 8g, protein 10g, salt 0.9g

Winter minestrone

. . . .

This is a real crowd-pleaser. Instead of cabbage, you could use kale, spinach, broccoli or shredded Brussels sprouts. Any leftover soup will keep in the fridge for up to 2 days.

🕐 PREP 15 mins COOK 40 mins   4

- 2 tbsp olive oil
- 1 onion, chopped
- 100g/4oz unsmoked lardons or chopped streaky bacon
- 2 large carrots, chopped
- 2 celery sticks, chopped
- 1 medium potato, chopped
- 2 garlic cloves, finely chopped or crushed
- 400g can chopped tomatoes
- 1 litre/1¾ pints vegetable stock (from granules or a cube)
- 2 tsp chopped sage leaves, or 1 tsp dried
- few cabbage leaves, shredded
- 400g can haricot beans
- handful chopped parsley

1 Heat the olive oil in a large pan, add the onion and lardons or bacon and fry for about 5 mins until the onion is starting to brown. Tip in the carrot, celery, potato and garlic, stir well and cook for a few minutes.

2 Add the tomatoes, stock and sage, and bring to the boil, stirring. Reduce the heat to simmer and cook partly covered for 30 mins, stirring in the cabbage after 15 mins. Drain and rinse the beans and add to the pan with the chopped parsley. Season and serve with crusty bread.

. . . .

PER SERVING 274 kcals, fat 13g, saturates 3g, carbs 28g, sugars 12g, fibre 8g, protein 13g, salt 2.56g

Hearty pasta soup

This speedy low-fat supper only takes 5 mins to prepare and is really filling. It counts as 3 of your 5-a-day and is the perfect midweek staple.

🕐 PREP 5 mins COOK 25 mins 4

- 1 tbsp olive oil
- 2 carrots, chopped
- 1 large onion, finely chopped
- 1 litre/1¾ pints vegetable stock
- 400g can chopped tomatoes with garlic
- 200g/7oz frozen mixed peas and beans
- 250g pack fresh filled pasta (we used tortellini with ricotta and spinach)
- handful basil leaves, chopped (optional)
- grated Parmesan, to serve

1 Heat the oil in a pan. Fry the carrots and onion for 5 mins until starting to soften. Add the stock and tomatoes, then simmer for 10 mins. Add the peas and beans with 5 mins to go.

2 Once the veg is tender, stir in the pasta. Return to the boil and simmer for 2 mins until the pasta is just cooked. Stir in the basil, if using. Season, then serve in bowls topped with a sprinkling of Parmesan and slices of garlic bread.

PER SERVING 286 kcals, fat 9g, saturates 3g, carbs 44g, sugars 11g, fibre 6g, protein 11g, salt 0.88g

Cauliflower cheese soup

Soup and cauliflower cheese are great comfort foods and this is a great combination of the two. Serve it in mugs for the perfect cosy night on the sofa.

 PREP 10 mins COOK 35 mins   6

- knob of butter
- 1 large onion, finely chopped
- 1 large cauliflower (about 900g/2lb), leaves trimmed and cut into florets
- 1 potato, peeled and cut into chunks
- 700ml/1¼ pints vegetable stock (from a cube is fine)
- 400ml/14fl oz milk
- 100g/4oz mature cheddar, diced

1 Heat the butter in a large saucepan. Tip in the onion and cook until softened, about 5 mins, stirring often. Add the cauliflower, potato, stock, milk and seasoning. Bring to the boil, then reduce the heat and leave to simmer for about 30 mins until the cauliflower is soft and the potato almost collapsing.

2 Whizz in a food processor or crush with a potato masher until you get a creamy, thick soup. Top up with more milk to thin a little if serving in mugs. You can make ahead up to 2 days in advance, cool, cover and leave in the fridge until needed, or freeze for up to 1 month. When ready to serve, warm through, ladle into mugs or bowls, top with the cheese pieces, then stir through before eating.

PER SERVING 188 kcals, fat 10g, saturates 5g, carbs 13g, sugars 9g, fibre 3g, protein 13g, salt 0.82g

Hearty winter veg soup

This soup ticks all the boxes. It's high in fibre, a good source of calcium, folic acid and vitamin C, counts as 3 of 5-a-day, and is low fat!

PREP 5 mins COOK 25 mins 4

- 1 tbsp olive oil
- 2 garlic cloves, crushed
- 1 swede, peeled and cut into chunks
- 4 large carrots, peeled and cut into chunks
- 3 sprigs thyme, leaves removed and roughly chopped
- 850ml/1½ pints vegetable stock
- 500ml/18fl oz semi-skimmed milk
- 2 x 410g cans mixed beans in water, drained

1 Heat the oil in a large saucepan, then gently soften the garlic without colouring. Tip in the swede, carrots and two-thirds of the thyme, then pour in the stock and milk. Bring to the boil, then simmer for 15 mins.

2 Ladle a third of the soup into a blender, whizz until smooth, then pour back into the pan along with the beans. Check for seasoning, then return to the heat and warm through. Serve sprinkled with the remaining thyme and some warm, crusty bread rolls.

PER SERVING 307 kcals, fat 7g, saturates 2g, carbs 47g, sugars 27g, fibre 14g, protein 17g, salt 0.99g

Chunky cheddar & celeriac soup

This is a hug in a bowl. Eat it with a gutsy salad (watercress is really good) or enjoy as a packed lunch as it reheats perfectly.

 PREP 15 mins COOK 40 mins 4

- 1 tbsp butter
- 3 onions, finely sliced
- 500g/1lb 2oz floury potatoes, peeled and diced
- 2 celeriac (1kg/2lb 4oz in total), peeled and diced
- 1 litre/1¾ pints chicken or vegetable stock (from a cube is fine)
- 4 sage leaves
- 2 strips lemon peel
- 200g/7oz mature cheddar, diced

1 In a large pan, melt the butter. Add the onion and cook for 5 mins until softened, but not coloured. Add the potato, celeriac, stock, sage and lemon peel. Bring to the boil and simmer gently for about 30 mins, until the celeriac is tender and the potato is collapsing. Remove and discard the lemon zest and sage leaves. Stir so the potato thickens the soup a little. (At this point you can cool and keep covered in the fridge for up to 2 days or freeze for up to 3 months.)

2 When you're ready to eat, reheat the soup to just simmering. Stir in the cheese.

PER SERVING 411 kcals, fat 22g, saturates 13g, carbs 35g, sugars 0g, fibre 12g, protein 21g, salt 2.40g

French onion soup

. . . .

This soup is an indulgent treat, but it's worth it. Make sure you caramelise the onions so that they have a rich flavour and are meltingly tender.

PREP 15 mins COOK 55 mins 4

- 50g/2oz butter
- 1 tbsp olive oil
- 1kg/2lb 4oz onions, halved and thinly sliced
- 1 tsp sugar
- 4 garlic cloves, thinly sliced
- 2 tbsp plain flour
- 250ml/9fl oz dry white wine
- 1.3 litres/2¼ pints hot strongly flavoured beef stock
- 4-8 slices French bread (depending on size)
- 140g/5oz Gruyère, finely grated

1 Melt the butter with the oil in a large heavy-based pan. Add the onion and fry with the lid on for 10 mins until soft. Sprinkle in the sugar and cook for 20 mins more, stirring frequently, until caramelised. The onion should be really golden, full of flavour and soft when pinched between your fingers. Take care towards the end to ensure that it doesn't burn.

2 Add the garlic for the final few mins of the onions' cooking time, then sprinkle in the flour and stir well. Increase the heat and keep stirring as you gradually add the wine, followed by the hot stock. Cover and simmer for 15-20 mins.

3 To serve, turn on the grill, and toast the bread. Ladle the soup into heatproof bowls. Put a slice or 2 of toast on top of the bowls of soup, and pile on the cheese. Grill until melted. Alternatively, you can complete the toasts under the grill, then serve them on top.

. . . .

PER SERVING 618 kcals, fat 27g, saturates 14g, carbs 59g, sugars 17g, fibre 9g, protein 26g, salt 2.6g

Neeps & tatties soup

This warming soup makes for a delicious starter when you're entertaining guests.

⏱ PREP 15 mins COOK 35 mins   🥧 2 for lunch or 4 as a starter

- 25g/1oz butter
- ¼ tsp ground coriander
- 1 onion, chopped
- ½ medium-sized swede (about 200g/7oz), peeled and chopped into small pieces
- 1 carrot, sliced
- 1 celery stick, sliced into small pieces
- 140g/5oz potatoes, chopped into small pieces
- good grating of nutmeg
- 400ml/14fl oz milk
- 140g/5oz cooked haggis or black pudding, chopped or crumbled into pieces
- 2 tbsp double cream
- a few celery leaves, torn

1 Melt the butter in a large saucepan over a medium heat. Add the coriander and the vegetables, fry for 4-5 mins, then cover with 400ml/14fl oz water and bring to the boil. Cook until all the vegetables are soft – around 20-25 mins.

2 Season with salt, pepper and nutmeg, then add the milk. Transfer to a blender or blitz with a stick blender until smooth, then return to the pan to heat through. (For a really smooth consistency, push the mixture through a sieve after blending.) Check the seasoning and add a little more salt and nutmeg, if you like.

3 Meanwhile, heat the cooked haggis or black pudding in a frying pan until sizzling. Serve the soup in bowls and top with the haggis or black pudding, a swirl of double cream and the celery leaves.

PER SERVING 260 kcals, fat 15g, saturates 7g, carbs 22g, sugars 9g, fibre 3g, protein 9g, salt 1.0g

Spiced citrus bean soup

The subtle creaminess of this soup makes it all the more filling and it is a great vegetarian lunch.

 PREP 15 mins COOK 30 mins 4

- 2 tbsp olive oil
- 2 onions, sliced
- 450g/1lb carrots, roughly chopped
- 1 tbsp garam masala
- finger-length piece ginger, grated
- juice 1 orange
- 1 litre/1¾ pints vegetable stock
- 200ml can reduced-fat coconut milk
- 410g can mixed beans, drained, rinsed
- 2 tbsp chopped coriander

1 Heat the oil in a large saucepan. Gently cook the onion and carrot for 15 mins until soft and golden. Add the garam masala and ginger, then cook for 1 min more.

2 Add the orange juice and stock, then bring to the boil. Simmer for 10 mins until the carrot is tender, then stir in the coconut milk. Using a stick blender, purée until smooth, then add the beans. Bring to a simmer, scatter over the coriander and serve.

PER SERVING 261 kcals, fat 13g, saturates 5g, carbs 31g, sugars 17g, fibre 9g, protein 9g, salt 1.15g

Alkalising green soup

This low-fat, gluten-free soup fights off colds and boosts your energy, as turmeric is a natural stimulant.

PREP 15 mins COOK 20 mins 2

- 1 tbsp sunflower oil
- 2 garlic cloves, sliced
- thumb-sized piece ginger, sliced
- ½ tsp ground coriander
- 3cm/1in piece fresh turmeric root, peeled and grated, or ½ tsp ground turmeric
- pinch of pink Himalayan salt
- 200g/7oz courgettes, roughly sliced
- 500ml/18fl oz stock, made by mixing 1 tbsp bouillon powder and boiling water in a jug
- 85g/3oz broccoli, chopped
- 100g/4oz kale, chopped
- zest and juice of 1 lime
- small pack parsley, roughly chopped, reserving a few whole leaves to serve

1 Put the oil in a deep pan, add the garlic, ginger, coriander, turmeric and salt, fry over a medium heat for 2 mins, then add 3 tbsp water to give a bit more moisture to the spice mixture.

2 Add the courgette slices, making sure you mix well to coat the slices in all the spices, and continue cooking for about 3 mins. Add 400ml/14fl oz of the stock and leave to simmer for 3 mins.

3 Add the broccoli, kale and lime juice with the rest of the stock. Leave to cook again for another 3-4 mins until all the vegetables are soft.

4 Take off the heat and add the chopped parsley. Pour everything into a blender and blend on high speed until smooth. It will be a beautiful green with bits of dark speckled through (which is the kale). Garnish with lime zest and parsley.

PER SERVING 182 kcals, fat 8g, saturates 1g, carbs 14g, sugars 4g, fibre 5g, protein 10g, salt 0.7g

Haddock & sweetcorn soup

Warm up with this delicious smoky and veg-packed soup. Replace smoked haddock with any other white fish you like if you want a more mellow-flavoured soup.

 PREP 10 mins COOK 20 mins 4

- 3 medium potatoes, chopped
- 600ml/1 pint full-fat milk
- 500ml/18fl oz hot fish stock
- 400g/14oz skinless smoked haddock fillet, cut into large chunks
- 200g/7oz broccoli, chopped
- 2 x 198g cans sweetcorn, drained
- squeeze lemon juice
- 2 spring onions, thinly sliced

1 Put the potatoes into a large saucepan with the milk and stock. Bring to the boil, then simmer for about 10 mins until tender. Mash some of the potatoes into the liquid.

2 Stir in the haddock and broccoli, then simmer for 5 mins until the fish is flaky and the broccoli is just tender. Stir in the sweetcorn and lemon juice, then warm through. Scatter over the spring onions to serve.

PER SERVING 360 kcals, fat 8g, saturates 4g, carbs 43g, sugars 16g, fibre 4g, protein 31g, salt 3.63g

Asparagus soup

This low-fat soup tastes its best when British asparagus is in season. You could swap the shallots for leeks and the asparagus for purple sprouting broccoli in the winter.

🕐 PREP 10 mins COOK 20 mins   4

- 25g/1oz butter
- a little vegetable oil
- 350g/12oz asparagus spears, stalks chopped, woody ends discarded, tips reserved
- 3 shallots, finely sliced
- 2 garlic cloves, crushed
- 2 large handfuls spinach
- 700ml/1¼ pints vegetable stock (fresh if possible)
- olive oil (optional), for drizzling

1 Heat the butter and oil in a large saucepan until foaming. Fry the asparagus tips for a few mins to soften. Remove and set aside.

2 Add the shallots, asparagus stalks and garlic, and cook for 5-10 mins until softened but still bright. Stir through the spinach, pour over the veg stock, bring to the boil, then blitz with a stick blender.

3 Season generously and add hot water to loosen if needed. Ladle into bowls and scatter the asparagus tips over each. Drizzle with olive oil and serve with sourdough bread, if you like.

PER SERVING 101 kcals, fat 8g, saturates 4g, carbs 4g, sugars 4g, fibre 4g, protein 4g, salt 0.6g

Hearty mushroom soup
· ·

Porcini mushrooms are packed with umami and add real depth to this super healthy, low-fat and satisfying soup.

🕐 PREP 30 mins COOK 30 mins   4-6

- 25g pack porcini mushrooms
- 2 tbsp olive oil
- 1 medium onion, finely diced
- 2 large carrots, diced
- 2 garlic cloves, finely chopped
- 1 tbsp chopped rosemary, or 1 tsp dried
- 500g/1lb 2oz fresh mushrooms, such as chestnut, finely chopped
- 1.2 litres/2 pints vegetable stock (from a cube is fine)
- 5 tbsp Marsala or dry sherry
- 2 tbsp tomato purée
- 100g/4oz pearl barley
- grated Parmesan (optional), to serve

1 Put the porcini in a bowl with 250ml/9fl oz boiling water and leave to soak for 25 mins. Heat the oil in a pan and add the onion, carrot, garlic, rosemary and seasoning. Fry for 5 mins on a medium heat until softened. Drain the porcini, saving the liquid, and finely chop. Tip into the pan with the fresh mushrooms. Fry for another 5 mins, then add the stock, Marsala or sherry, tomato purée, barley and strained porcini liquid.

2 Cook for 30 mins or until barley is soft, adding more liquid if it becomes a little too thick. Serve in bowls with the Parmesan sprinkled over, if desired.

· ·
PER SERVING 245 kcals, fat 7g, saturates 1g, carbs 35g, sugars 10g, fibre 3g, protein 8g, salt 1.13g

Beef goulash soup

. . . .

This low-fat meaty soup is packed full of veg, providing 3 of your 5-a-day with loads of vitamin C.

🕐 PREP 15 mins COOK 1 hr   🥧 2-3

- 1 tbsp rapeseed oil
- 1 large onion, halved and sliced
- 3 garlic cloves, sliced
- 200g/7oz extra-lean stewing beef, finely diced
- 1 tsp caraway seeds
- 2 tsp smoked paprika
- 400g can chopped tomatoes
- 600ml/1 pint beef stock
- 1 medium sweet potato, peeled and diced
- 1 green pepper, deseeded and diced

SUPERCHARGED TOPPING
- 150g pot natural bio yogurt
- good handful parsley, chopped

1 Heat the oil in a large pan, add the onion and garlic, and fry for 5 mins until starting to colour. Stir in the beef, increase the heat and fry, stirring, to brown it.

2 Add the caraway and paprika, stir well, then tip in the tomatoes and stock. Cover and leave to cook gently for 30 mins.

3 Stir in the sweet potato and green pepper, cover and cook for 20 mins more or until tender. Allow to cool a little, then serve topped with the yogurt and parsley (if the soup is too hot, it will kill the beneficial bacteria in the yogurt).

. . . .
PER SERVING (3) 345 kcals, fat 12g, saturates 4g, carbs 28g, sugars 18g, fibre 7g, protein 25g, salt 1.0g

Moroccan tomato & chickpea soup with couscous

The couscous makes this fragrant and spicy soup more filling for a satisfying vegetarian supper.

 PREP 20 mins COOK 45 mins 4

- 75g/3oz couscous
- 3 tbsp olive oil
- 750ml/1½ pints hot vegetable stock
- 1 large onion, finely chopped
- 1 carrot, chopped into small cubes
- 4 garlic cloves, crushed
- ½ finger piece ginger, peeled and finely chopped
- 1-2 tbsp ras-el-hanout
- 1 tbsp harissa paste, plus extra to serve
- 400g tin chopped tomatoes
- 400g tin chickpeas
- juice ½ lemon
- roughly chopped coriander, to serve

1 Tip the couscous into a bowl, season with salt and pepper and stir through 1 tbsp of the oil. Pour over enough hot stock just to cover and cover the bowl with cling film and set aside.

2 Heat the rest of the oil in a saucepan and cook the onion and carrot gently for 8 mins until softened. Add the garlic and ginger and cook for 2 mins more then stir in the ras el hanout and harissa and cook for another minute. Pour in the tomatoes and remaining stock and give everything a good stir. Season, add the chickpeas and simmer everything gently for 20 mins until thickened slightly, then squeeze over the lemon.

3 Uncover the couscous and fluff up with a fork. Spoon the soup into bowls, top each with a mound of couscous, scatter with coriander and serve with extra harissa for those who want it.

PER SERVING 265 kcals, fat 10.4 g, saturates 1.4g, carbs 33g, sugars 10g, fibre 6g, protein 7.3g, salt 1.2 g

Spiced root soup with crisp spiced onions

· ·

The carrots add sweetness to this root vegetable soup, while the spices add a subtle heat. It also freezes well, so it's worth making double.

PREP 20 mins COOK 45 mins 4

- 2 onions
- 3 tbsp vegetable oil
- 1 tsp mustard seeds
- 1 tsp cumin seeds
- 2 leeks, sliced
- 3 carrots, sliced
- 2 medium potatoes, chopped
- 2 parsnips or 1 small celeriac, chopped
- 2-3 tsp curry paste
- 1.2 litres/2 pints vegetable stock (from granules or a cube)
- 250ml/9fl oz natural yogurt, plus extra to serve
- coriander or parsley, roughly chopped, to finish

1 Peel and halve the onions through the root, then slice thinly lengthways. Heat 2 tbsp of the oil in a large pan, add half the onions and fry until just starting to colour. Add the mustard and cumin seeds and fry until they are nicely browned.

2 Add the vegetables and curry paste and stir until well coated. Pour in the stock and bring to the boil. Reduce the heat, partly cover and simmer for 30 mins, until the vegetables are tender. Meanwhile, heat the remaining tbsp of oil in a small pan, add the remaining onion and fry quickly until crisp and browned. Tip onto kitchen paper.

3 Purée the soup in batches, then return to the pan and stir in most of the yogurt. Taste and add salt, if necessary. Reheat gently, then ladle into bowls and top each with a spoonful of yogurt, some fried onions and a scattering of roughly chopped coriander or parsley.

· ·

PER SERVING 240 kcals, fat 13g, saturates 1g, carbs 25g, sugars 16g, fibre 7g, protein 9g, salt 1.45g

Courgette, potato & cheddar soup

This super healthy soup is a great source of vitamin C. It's quick and easy to prepare and you can pick up all the ingredients from your local supermarket.

PREP 15 mins COOK 15 mins 8

- 500g/1lb 2oz potatoes, unpeeled and roughly chopped
- 2 vegetable stock cubes
- 1kg/2lb 4oz courgettes, roughly chopped
- bunch spring onions, sliced – save 1 for serving, if eating straight away
- 100g/4oz extra-mature cheddar or vegetarian alternative, grated, plus a little extra to serve
- good grating fresh nutmeg, plus extra to serve

1 Put the potatoes in a large pan with just enough water to cover them and crumble in the stock cubes. Bring to the boil, then cover and cook for 5 mins. Add the courgettes, put the lid back on and cook for 5 mins more. Throw in the spring onions, cover and cook for a final 5 mins.

2 Take off the heat, then stir in the cheese and season with the nutmeg, salt and pepper. Whizz to a thick soup, adding more hot water until you get the consistency you like. Serve scattered with extra grated cheddar, spring onions and nutmeg or pepper. Or cool and freeze in freezer bags or containers with good lids for up to 3 months.

PER SERVING 131 kcals, fat 6g, saturates 3g, carbs 14g, sugars 3g, fibre 2g, protein 7g, salt 1.31g

Turkey minestrone

A low-fat, warm and comforting soup for wintry days. You could add a drizzle of extra virgin olive oil and some grated Parmesan, if you like.

 PREP 15 mins COOK 40 mins   6

- 2 tsp olive oil
- 100g/4oz smoked bacon lardons
- 1 red onion, finely chopped
- 1 carrot, finely chopped
- 1 celery stick, finely chopped
- 2 garlic cloves, finely chopped
- 2 bay leaves
- 2 thyme sprigs
- 300g/11oz celeriac (or any other root veg), cut into cubes
- 200g/7oz potato, cut into cubes
- 400g can borlotti beans, drained and rinsed
- 1.5 litres/2¾ pints turkey or chicken stock (fresh is best)
- 350g/12oz cooked turkey
- 100g/4oz orzo
- 75g/2½oz curly kale, shredded

1 Heat 1 tsp of oil in a large saucepan. Add the bacon and fry over a medium-to-high heat for 4-5 mins or until golden, then set aside.

2 Put the remaining oil, the onion, carrot, celery and a pinch of salt in the pan. Cook gently over a low heat for 8-10 mins, stirring occasionally, until the veg is soft but not coloured. Add the garlic and herbs, and cook for 2 mins more.

3 Tip in the celeriac, potato, borlotti beans and chicken stock. Bring to the boil, then simmer, uncovered, for 10-15 mins. Add the cooked turkey, orzo and the bacon, and cook for 10 mins.

4 Just before serving, tip in the kale, give everything a good stir and return to the heat for about 2 mins or until the kale has wilted.

PER SERVING 345 kcals, fat 8g, saturates 3g, carbs 28g, sugars 4g, fibre 8g, protein 36g, salt 1.5g

Roasted sweet potato & carrot soup

Packed full of fibre, this soup has smoky undertones from roasting the sweet potatoes and carrots. It provides 2 of your 5-a-day too!

 PREP 15 mins COOK 35 mins 4

- 500g/1lb 2oz sweet potatoes, peeled and cut into chunks
- 300g/11oz carrots, peeled and cut into chunks
- 3 tbsp olive oil
- 2 onions, finely chopped
- 2 garlic cloves, crushed
- 1 litre/1¾ pints vegetable stock
- 100ml/3½fl oz crème fraîche, plus extra to serve

1 Heat oven to 220C/200C fan/ gas 7 and put the sweet potato and carrot into a large roasting tin, drizzled with 2 tbsp olive oil and plenty of seasoning. Roast the vegetables in the oven for 25-30 mins or until caramelised and tender.

2 Meanwhile, put the remaining 1 tbsp olive oil in a large deep saucepan and fry the onion over a medium-low heat for about 10 mins until softened. Add the garlic and stir for 1 min before adding the stock. Simmer for 5-10 mins until the onion is very soft, then set aside.

3 Once the roasted veg is done, leave to cool a little, then transfer to the saucepan and use a stick blender to process until smooth. Stir in the crème fraîche, a little more seasoning and reheat until hot. Serve in bowls topped with a swirl of crème fraîche and a good grinding of black pepper.

PER SERVING 419 kcals, fat 19g, saturates 8g, carbs 45g, sugars 27g, fibre 10g, protein 11g, salt 0.9g

Lentil & bacon soup

Lentils are a great source of protein and are slow releasing to help you feel fuller for longer. This soup is so easy to make and is packed full of flavour.

PREP 5 mins COOK 35 mins 3

- 1 tbsp olive oil
- 1 onion, diced
- 2 x 70g packs pancetta cubes
- 1 carrot, finely diced
- 1 tsp ground cumin
- ½ tsp turmeric
- 2 garlic cloves, finely chopped
- 1 chilli, sliced
- 2 low-sodium stock cubes
- 250g red lentils, rinsed

1 Heat the olive oil in a large saucepan. Add the onion, 1 pack of pancetta and the carrot. Cook on a low to medium heat for 10 minutes until the onion is soft.
2 Add the cumin, turmeric, garlic and chilli and cook for a further 1-2 minutes until the aromas are released.
3 Pour in 1.25 litres/2¼ pints of boiling water, crumble in the stock cubes and add the lentils. Bring to a simmer and cook for 20 mins, stirring occasionally to ensure the lentils aren't sticking.
4 Meanwhile, fry the remaining lardons in a small frying pan for about 10 minutes until crispy. You don't need to add any oil as plenty will run from the pancetta.
5 Serve the soup with a sprinkle of crispy lardons on top.

PER SERVING 493 kcals, fat 19g, saturates 6.6g, carbs 51g, sugars 7.3g, fibre 8g, protein 29.5g, salt 1.6g

Red lentil, chickpea & chilli soup

The addition of red lentils and chickpeas to this veggie soup means you will feel fuller for longer. Replace the chickpeas with another pulse like butter beans, if you like.

PREP 10 mins COOK 25 mins 4

- 2 tsp cumin seeds
- large pinch chilli flakes
- 1 tbsp olive oil
- 1 red onion, chopped
- 140g/5oz red split lentils
- 850ml/1½ pints vegetable stock or water
- 400g can tomatoes, whole or chopped
- 200g carton chickpeas or ½ a can, rinsed and drained
- small bunch coriander, roughly chopped (save a few leaves, to serve)
- 4 tbsp 0% Greek yogurt, to serve

1 Heat a large saucepan and dry-fry the cumin seeds and chilli flakes for 1 min, or until they start to jump around the pan and release their aromas. Add the oil and onion, and cook for 5 mins. Stir in the lentils, stock and tomatoes, then bring to the boil. Simmer for 15 mins until the lentils have softened.

2 Whizz the soup with a stick blender or in a food processor until it is a rough purée, pour back into the pan and add the chickpeas. Heat gently, season well and stir in the coriander. Finish with a dollop of yogurt and coriander leaves.

PER SERVING 222 kcals, fat 5g, saturates 0g, carbs 33g, sugars 6g, fibre 6g, protein 13g, salt 0.87g

Bean & barley soup

This low-fat soup is full of vitamin C, fibre and iron. It is so quick to prepare and then simmers away while you put your feet up. It is full of flavour and freezes well too.

PREP 5 mins COOK 1 hour 4

- 2 tbsp vegetable oil
- 1 large onion, finely chopped
- 1 fennel bulb, quartered, cored and sliced
- 5 garlic cloves, crushed
- 400g can chickpeas, drained and rinsed
- 2 x 400g cans chopped tomatoes
- 600ml/1 pint vegetable stock
- 250g/9oz pearl barley
- 215g can butter beans, drained and rinsed
- 100g pack baby spinach leaves
- grated Parmesan, to serve

1 Heat the oil in a saucepan over a medium heat, add the onion, fennel and garlic, and cook until softened and just beginning to brown, about 10-12 mins.

2 Mash half the chickpeas and add to the pan with the tomatoes, stock and barley. Top up with a can of water and bring to the boil, then reduce the heat and simmer, covered, for 45 mins or until the barley is tender. Add another can of water if the liquid has significantly reduced.

3 Add the remaining chickpeas and the butter beans to the soup. After a few mins, stir in the spinach and cook until wilted, about 1 min. Season and serve scattered with Parmesan.

PER SERVING 488 kcals, fat 9g, saturates 1g, carbs 78g, sugars 11g, fibre 12g, protein 16g, salt 1.4g

Red lentil & coconut soup

This creamy veggie soup is so fragrant and warming, using turmeric, ginger and coconut milk.

PREP 5 mins COOK 30 mins 4

- 100g/4oz red lentils
- 1 heaped tsp turmeric
- 1 tbsp coarsely grated ginger
- 2 garlic cloves, sliced
- 1 litre/1¾ pints vegetable stock
- 400ml can coconut milk
- 2 leeks, well washed and sliced
- 2 handfuls baby spinach (approx 50g/2oz)

SUPERCHARGED TOPPING
- 2 limes, cut into wedges

1 Tip the lentils into a large pan and add the turmeric, ginger and garlic. Pour in the stock, then cover the pan and simmer for 15 mins until the lentils have softened.

2 Pour in the coconut milk, stir in the leek, cover and cook for 10 mins more.

3 Add the spinach and cook just to wilt it, then spoon into bowls and squeeze over the lime juice to serve.

PER SERVING 314 kcals, fat 19g, saturates 15g, carbs 22g, sugars 6g, fibre 6g, protein 10g, salt 0.7g

Spiced black bean & chicken soup with kale

....

Wholesome and hearty, this South American-style soup is low fat, full of fibre and vitamin C and provides 2 of your 5-a-day.

🕐 PREP 10 mins COOK 15 mins 4

- 2 tbsp mild olive oil
- 2 fat garlic cloves, crushed
- small bunch coriander, stalks finely chopped, leaves picked
- zest 1 lime, then cut into wedges
- 2 tsp ground cumin
- 1 tsp chilli flakes
- 400g can chopped tomatoes 400g can black beans, rinsed and drained
- 600ml/1 pint chicken stock
- 175g/6oz kale, thick stalks removed, leaves shredded
- 250g/9oz leftover roast or ready-cooked chicken
- 50g/2oz feta, crumbled, and flour & corn tortillas, toasted, to serve

1 Heat the oil in a large saucepan, add the garlic, coriander stalks and lime zest, then fry for 2 mins until fragrant. Stir in the cumin and chilli flakes, fry for 1 min more, then tip in the tomatoes, beans and stock. Bring to the boil, then crush the beans against the bottom of the pan a few times using a potato masher. This will thicken the soup a little.

2 Stir the kale into the soup, simmer for 5 mins or until tender, then tear in the chicken and let it heat through. Season with salt, pepper and juice from half the lime, then serve in shallow bowls, scattered with the feta and a few coriander leaves. Serve the remaining lime in wedges for the table, with the toasted tortillas on the side. The longer you leave the chicken in the pan, the thicker the soup will become, so add a splash more stock if you can't serve the soup straight away.

....

PER SERVING 293kcals, fat 11g, saturates 2g, carbs 15g, sugars 3g, fibre 6g, protein 29g, salt 1.0g

Mexican chicken & wild rice soup

This easy feel-good soup is the perfect after-work supper and is super healthy too. It counts as 2 of your 5-a-day, is low fat and a great source of vitamin C.

PREP 10 mins COOK 20 mins 4

- 1 tsp olive oil
- 1 onion, finely chopped
- 1 green pepper, diced
- 200g/7oz sweetcorn, frozen or from a can
- 1-2 tbsp chipotle paste (we used Discovery)
- 250g pouch ready-cooked long-grain and wild rice mix
- 400g can black beans in water, rinsed and drained
- 1.3 litres/2¼ pints low-sodium chicken stock
- 2 cooked skinless chicken breasts, shredded
- small bunch coriander, chopped
- low-fat soured cream and reduced-fat guacamole, to serve, if you like

1 Heat the oil in a large non-stick frying pan and cook the onion for 5 mins. Throw in the pepper and cook for 2 mins more, then add the sweetcorn, chipotle paste and rice. Stir well and cook for 1-2 mins.

2 Add the black beans and the stock. Bring to the boil, turn down to a simmer, then add half the chicken and coriander. Cook for 2-3 mins, then ladle into bowls.

3 Scatter over the rest of the chicken and coriander. Serve with a dollop each of guacamole and soured cream on top if you like.

PER SERVING 347 kcals, fat 7g, saturates 1g, carbs 45g, sugars 5g, fibre 5g, protein 29g, salt 0.48g

Spicy chilli bean soup

This Mexican-inspired soup is high in fibre, low in fat and 3 of your 5-a-day. If you like spice, use hot chilli powder instead of mild for a real kick!

PREP 10 mins COOK 40 mins 4

- 1 tbsp olive oil
- 1 large onion, finely chopped
- 1 garlic clove, crushed
- 1 tbsp tomato purée
- 1 tsp mild chilli powder
- ½ tsp ground cumin
- 400g can chopped tomatoes
- 500ml/18fl oz vegetable stock
- 400g can mixed beans, drained and rinsed
- 1 red pepper, cut into chunky dice
- tortilla chips, to serve
- 4 lime wedges, to serve

1 Heat the oil in a deep saucepan and fry the chopped onion over a medium heat until tender. Add the garlic and tomato purée, stirring for 1-2 mins until combined. Sprinkle in the spices and cook for another 1 min.

2 Tip in the chopped tomatoes, half fill the can with water, and add to the pan. Pour in the stock and simmer on a medium heat for 10-15 mins, uncovered. Season, then whizz using a stick blender until smooth. Add the beans and red pepper, and cook for another 15 mins until the pepper is tender.

3 Serve in bowls topped with a small pile of tortilla chips and a lime wedge.

PER SERVING 157 kcals, fat 4g, saturates 0g, carbs 18g, sugars 10g, fibre 9g, protein 8g, salt 0.5g

Porcini, pancetta & spelt soup

This Tuscan-inspired soup has a rich flavour from the porcini mushrooms and tastes delicious with the bacon. It's all cooked in one pan, so less washing up too.

⏱ PREP 15 mins COOK 45-50 mins   4

- 50g/2oz pancetta cubes (or bacon)
- 1 tbsp olive oil
- 1 bay leaf
- 1 onion, finely chopped
- 1 garlic clove, crushed
- 1 litre/1¾ pints vegetable stock
- 140g/5oz pearled spelt (or farro)
- small handful dried porcini mushrooms, crumbled
- 2 tomatoes, skinned, deseeded and diced (or 2 whole tomatoes from a can, chopped)
- 6-8 small button mushrooms, quartered
- flat-leaf parsley and Parmesan, to serve

1 Fry the pancetta in the oil for 2-3 mins in a medium saucepan. Add the bay leaf and onion. Cook over a gentle heat until the onion is soft and translucent. Add the garlic, fry for a few secs more, then pour over the stock and bring to the boil. Rinse the spelt and drain well. Add to the stock along with the porcini and tomatoes, then simmer very gently for 25-30 mins.

2 Add the button mushrooms and simmer for 10 mins more, or until the grains are tender. Season with salt and freshly ground pepper. Ladle the soup into bowls, then sprinkle with parsley and freshly grated Parmesan.

PER SERVING 220 kcals, fat 8g, saturates 2g, carbs 30g, sugars 8g, fibre 4g, protein 10g, salt 1.30g

Spicy harissa, aubergine & chickpea soup

. . . .

Spicy and smoky – this soup is full of Middle Eastern flavours and is low fat and 3 of your 5-a-day.

PREP 10 mins COOK 40 mins 4

- 1 onion, chopped
- 1 tbsp olive oil
- 2 tbsp harissa
- 2 aubergines, diced
- 400g can chopped tomatoes
- 400g can chickpeas, drained
- 2 tbsp coriander, chopped

1 Soften the onion in the olive oil in a large saucepan. Add the harissa and cook for 2 mins, stirring. Add the diced aubergine and coat in the harissa.

2 Add the chopped tomatoes, drained chickpeas and 500ml/18fl oz water. Bring to the boil and simmer for 30 mins. Stir through the chopped coriander, season and serve.

. . . .

PER SERVING 157 kcals, fat 5g, saturates 1g, carbs 20g, sugars 8g, fibre 9g, protein 6g, salt 0.7g

Herby chicken & butter bean soup

This is a great way to use up leftover chicken from a roast. It's low calorie and freezes well, so make the full batch and freeze the rest for up to 3 months.

PREP 20 mins COOK 1 hr 6

- 1 leftover chicken carcass plus 225g/8oz meat (thigh and leg meat is best), or 4 skinless chicken thighs, plus 1.5 litres/2¾ pints chicken stock
- 2 tbsp olive or rapeseed oil
- 2 onions, chopped
- 6 carrots, chopped
- 3-4 sprigs each rosemary, sage and thyme, leaves picked and chopped
- 2 tsp each ground cumin and coriander
- 1 tsp turmeric
- 1 tbsp plain flour
- 400g can butter beans, drained

1 If using a leftover carcass, place in a large saucepan and cover with 2 litres/3½ pints of water. Bring to the boil, then cover with a lid and gently simmer for 20 mins. Meanwhile, heat the oil in another large saucepan. If using chicken thighs, add these and brown on all sides, then remove and set aside.

2 Add the onion to the oil and cook for 10 mins until starting to caramelise. Add the carrot, herbs, spices and flour and stir for 1-2 mins to toast the spices. If using a carcass, strain the liquid into the pan with the veg, otherwise add the browned chicken thighs and stock. Stir well, cover and simmer for 30 mins.

3 If using chicken thighs, remove them from the pan, shred the meat and discard the bones. Add the meat (or the meat from the carcass) back into the soup, along with the butter beans, season and heat through for 1-2 mins.

4 Use a stick blender to blitz about half the soup, so it's creamy but still has chunks of chicken, carrot and butter bean. Serve with extra pepper, and good crusty bread.

PER SERVING 363 kcals, fat 19g, saturates 4g, carbs 19g, sugars 11g, fibre 7g, protein 32g, salt 0.8g

Springtime minestrone

· ·

This simple low-fat soup will become a favourite standby for a quick lunch.

🕐 PREP 5 mins COOK 5 mins   🥧 4

- 200g/8oz mixed green vegetables (we used asparagus, broad beans and spring onions)
- 700ml/1¼ pints hot vegetable stock
- 140g/5oz cooked pasta (spaghetti works well, chopped into small pieces)
- 215g can butter beans, rinsed and drained
- 3 tbsp green pesto

1 Place the green vegetables in a medium-sized saucepan, then pour over the stock. Bring to the boil, then reduce the heat and simmer until the vegetables are cooked through, about 3 mins. Stir in the cooked pasta, beans and 1 tbsp of pesto. Warm through, then ladle into bowls and top each with another drizzle of pesto.

· ·
PER SERVING 125 kcals, fat 4g, saturates 1g, carbs 16g, sugars 3g, fibre 4g, protein 8g, salt 0.7g

Caramelised onion & barley soup with cheese croutons

Barley adds a delicious nuttiness to this soup and is a great way to bulk up soups and stews instead of using rice or pasta.

PREP 10 mins COOK 35 mins 2

- 1 tbsp olive oil
- 2 medium onions, thinly sliced
- 2 garlic cloves, thinly sliced
- 6 thyme sprigs, chopped
- good pinch sugar
- 500ml/18fl oz vegetable stock
- 60g/2½oz barley
- 60g/2½oz cavolo nero or kale, thick stalks discarded and leaves sliced
- 4 slices baguette, toasted
- 4 tbsp grated Gruyère cheese

1 1 Heat the oil in a saucepan, then add the onions, garlic, thyme, sugar and a good pinch of salt. Cook on a medium-low heat for 15-20 mins or until golden coloured. Add the stock and simmer for a further 10 mins.

2 In a separate large saucepan of salted boiling water, cook the barley for 15 mins, adding the cavolo nero or kale for the final 3 mins of cooking. Drain and rinse under cold water, then add to the soup and warm through.

3 Heat the grill. Top the toasted bread with cheese and place under the grill until it's bubbly and melted. Serve in 2 large bowls with the cheesy croutons on top.

Chunky butternut mulligatawny

Warm up after a long walk with this filling soup. It's low fat, low calorie, full of fibre and vitamin C, as well as being gluten free.

PREP 25 mins COOK 40 mins 6

- 2 tbsp olive or rapeseed oil
- 2 onions, finely chopped
- 2 dessert apples, peeled and finely chopped
- 3 celery sticks, finely chopped
- ½ small butternut squash, peeled, seeds removed, chopped into small pieces
- 2-3 heaped tbsp curry powder (depending on how spicy you like it)
- 1 tbsp ground cinnamon
- 1 tbsp nigella seeds
- 2 x 400g cans chopped tomatoes
- 1.5 litres/2¾ pints chicken or vegetable stock
- 140g/5oz basmati rice
- small pack parsley, chopped
- 3 tbsp mango chutney, plus a little to serve, if you like
- natural yogurt, to serve

1 Heat the oil in your largest saucepan. Add the onions, apples and celery with a pinch of salt. Cook for 10 mins, stirring now and then, until softened. Add the butternut squash, curry powder, cinnamon, nigella seeds and a grind of black pepper. Cook for 2 mins more, then stir in the tomatoes and stock. Cover with a lid and simmer for 15 mins.

2 By now the vegetables should be tender. Stir in the rice, pop the lid back on and simmer for another 12 mins until the rice is cooked through. Taste and add more seasoning if needed. Stir through the parsley and mango chutney, then serve in bowls with yogurt and extra mango chutney on top, if you like.

PER SERVING 212 kcals, fat 5g, saturates 1g, carbs 37g, sugars 15g, fibre 6g, protein 6g, salt 0.5g

Courgette, pea & pesto soup

This soup is packed with veg, high in fibre, folic acid and is a great source of vitamin C. Feel revitalised and energised after a big bowl of this.

PREP 10 mins COOK 15 mins 4

- 1 tbsp olive oil
- 1 garlic clove, sliced
- 500g/1lb 2oz courgettes, quartered lengthways and chopped
- 200g/7oz frozen peas
- 400g can cannellini beans, drained and rinsed
- 1 litre/1¾ pints hot vegetable stock
- 2 tbsp basil pesto

1 Heat the oil in a large saucepan. Cook the garlic for a few secs, then add the courgettes and cook for 3 mins until they start to soften. Stir in the peas and cannellini beans, pour on the hot stock and cook for a further 3 mins.

2 Stir the pesto through the soup with some seasoning, then ladle into bowls and serve with crusty brown bread, if you like. Or pop in a flask to take to work.

PER SERVING 200 kcals, fat 8g, saturates 2g, carbs 21g, sugar 7g, fibre 8g, protein 12g, salt 1.05g

Merguez beanpot

Merguez sausages add a spicy flavour and rich colour to the soup, but if you are looking for something milder, then any good-quality sausage will work well, too.

🕐 PREP 10 mins COOK 45 mins 4

- 2 tbsp olive oil
- 500g/1lb 2oz merguez sausages, cut into bite-sized pieces
- 2 onions, chopped
- 1 red pepper, chopped
- 2 x 400g cans chopped tomatoes
- 2 tbsp each Worcestershire sauce, Dijon mustard and brown sugar
- 2 x 400g cans cannellini or red kidney beans, drained
- coriander or parsley and tortillas, to serve

1 Heat the oil in a large pan, add the sausages and fry until browned. Add the onion and pepper, and fry for 5 mins until softened. Add the tomatoes and 1 can of water, the Worcestershire sauce, mustard and sugar. Season and bring to the boil. Give it a stir, then reduce the heat, cover and simmer for 15 mins.

2 Stir in the beans, return to a simmer and cook for a further 5 mins. Scatter with parsley or coriander and serve in bowls with tortillas.

PER SERVING 658 kcals, fat 39g, saturates 12g, carbs 47g, sugar 28g, fibre 10g, protein 25g, salt 4.8g

Green bean minestrone

Using a selection of green veg gives the soup a summery feel; the beans make a nice texture contrast to the pasta and cabbage.

PREP 20 mins COOK 30 mins 4

- 1 onion, finely chopped
- 1 garlic clove, finely chopped
- 1 carrot, finely chopped
- 1 celery stick, finely chopped
- 2 tbsp olive oil
- 70g pack pancetta cubes (optional)
- 1 bay leaf
- 1.5 litres/2¾ pints vegetable or chicken stock
- 100g/4oz small pasta shapes, such as stelline or orzo
- 300g/11oz mixed runner, green and podded broad beans
- 100g/4oz spring cabbage, shredded
- 4 tbsp pesto

1 Fry the onion, garlic, carrot and celery in the olive oil in a large saucepan until tender but not browned. Scoop out and set aside. Fry the pancetta, if using, you won't need to add any more oil. Fry until browned but not too crisp. Tip into a sieve and drain off any excess fat. Put the carrot mixture back into the pan with the pancetta and add the bay leaf, plenty of seasoning and the stock. Bring to a simmer, add the pasta and cook for 5 mins.

2 Top and tail the green and runner beans, slice both into lengths that will easily fit on a spoon and add to the pot with the broad beans. Cook for 3 mins, then add the cabbage. Bring back to a simmer and cook for 2 mins. Spoon the pesto onto the top of the soup just before serving and serve with crusty bread.

PER SERVING 260 kcals, fat 11g, saturates 2g, carbs 31g, sugar 9g, fibre 6g, protein 10g, salt 1.13g

Chorizo & chickpea soup

For a spiced Indian version of this soup, you could add some cooked chicken and 1 tsp curry paste instead of the chorizo.

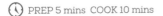 PREP 5 mins COOK 10 mins   2

- 400g can chopped tomatoes
- 110g pack of chorizo sausage (unsliced)
- 140g/5oz wedge Savoy cabbage
- sprinkling dried chilli flakes
- 410g can chickpeas, drained and rinsed
- 1 chicken or vegetable stock cube

1 Put a medium pan on the heat and tip in the tomatoes, followed by a can of water. While the tomatoes are heating, quickly chop the chorizo into chunky pieces (removing any skin) and shred the cabbage.

2 Pile the chorizo and cabbage into the pan with the chilli flakes and chickpeas, then crumble in the stock cube. Stir well, cover and leave to bubble over a high heat for 6 mins or until the cabbage is just tender. Ladle into bowls and eat with crusty or garlic bread.

PER SERVING 366 kcals, fat 18g, saturates 5g, carbs 30g, sugars 0g, fibre 9g, protein 23g, salt 4.26g

Hearty lamb & barley soup

This warming low fat soup counts as 2 of your 5-a-day. Add some chopped fresh parsley at the end if you like.

 PREP 10 mins COOK 30 mins 4

- 1 tsp olive oil
- 200g/7oz lamb neck fillet, trimmed of fat and cut into small pieces
- ½ large onion, finely chopped
- 50g/2oz pearl barley
- 600g/1lb 5oz mixed root vegetables
- 2 tsp Worcestershire sauce
- 1 litre/1¾ pints lamb or beef stock
- 1 thyme sprig
- 100g/4oz green beans (frozen are fine), finely chopped

1 Heat the oil in a large saucepan. Season the lamb, then fry for a few mins until browned. Add the onion and barley, then gently fry for 1 min. Add the veg, cook for 2 more mins, then add the Worcestershire sauce, stock and thyme. Cover, then simmer for 20 mins.

2 When everything is cooked, spoon about a quarter of the soup into a separate pan. Purée with a stick blender (or put into a normal blender and whizz), then stir it back into the rest of the soup. Add the green beans, simmer for 3 mins, then ladle the soup into bowls and serve with granary bread.

PER SERVING 258 kcals, fat 11g, saturates 4g, carbs 26g, sugars 12g, fibre 4g, protein 17g, salt 1.48g

Sausage minestrone

Bulk up this chunky vegetable soup with hearty sausage and cannellini beans for a filling mid-week lunch or dinner.

 PREP 20 mins COOK 40 mins 6

- 2 tbsp olive oil, plus extra for drizzling
- 2 onions, finely chopped
- 6 carrots, roughly diced
- 4 celery sticks, roughly diced
- 4 garlic cloves, roughly chopped
- 8 sausages, skin removed and sausage meat broken into walnut-sized pieces
- 1 tbsp tomato purée
- 2 x 400g cans chopped tomatoes
- 1 chicken stock cube, crumbled
- 400g can cannellini beans, drained and rinsed
- 1 tbsp golden caster sugar
- 1 tbsp red wine vinegar
- large pack parsley, roughly chopped
- toast and tapenade (optional), to serve

1 Put the oil, onion, carrot, celery and garlic in a large saucepan. Cook gently over a low heat for 15 mins or until soft. Meanwhile, tip the sausage pieces into a non-stick frying pan, turn up the heat and sizzle for a few mins to brown. Put to one side.

2 Stir tomato purée through the soft vegetables and cook for 1 min more. Pour in the tomatoes, 3½ cans of water and the stock cube. Stir and simmer for 10 mins. Add the sausage pieces and beans, and bubble down for 10 mins until the sausages are cooked through. Season and stir in the sugar, vinegar and parsley. Spoon into bowls, adding a slice of toast spread with tapenade to float, if you like, and a drizzle more olive oil, if you like.

PER SERVING 393 kcals, fat 23g, saturates 7g, carbs 32g, sugars 19g, fibre 6g, protein 14g, salt 2.4g

Broad bean, yogurt & mint soup

This soup turns out the most delectable pale green, so pretty when flecked with darker green mint. Don't reheat it once you've mixed in the yogurt – it will curdle!

PREP 20 mins COOK 30 mins 4

- 1 onion, chopped
- 1 stick of celery, thinly sliced
- 25g/1oz butter
- 2 tbsp risotto or pudding rice
- 1 generous sprig of summer savory or thyme
- 350g/12oz shelled broad beans (about 1.3kg/3lb before podding)
- 1 litre/1¾ pints chicken or vegetable stock, plus about 100ml/3½fl oz more if needed
- 100g/4oz shelled peas (about 350g/12oz before podding)

TO SERVE
- 7 tbsp Greek yogurt, plus extra
- 1 tbsp chopped mint leaves

1 Fry the onion and celery gently in the butter in a covered saucepan over a low heat for about 10 minutes until very tender. Tip in the rice, add the savory or thyme and cook for another minute, uncovered. Now add the broad beans, pour in 1 litre/1¾ pints stock and season. Bring to the boil, simmer for about 5 minutes, then tip in the peas and cook for a further 5 minutes, by which time the rice will be tender.

2 Remove the herb sprig and purée the soup in batches in a blender or food processor, then return to the rinsed-out pan.

3 Shortly before serving, reheat the soup thoroughly and add more stock if the consistency is too thick. Take the pan off the heat and stir in 1 tbsp of the yogurt and the chopped mint. Continue to stir in the yogurt, 1 tbsp at a time, until it's all incorporated. Taste for seasoning, then serve in bowls with an extra spoonful of yogurt stirred into each and a grinding of black pepper.

PER SERVING 194 kcals, fat 9g, saturates 5g, carbs 19g, sugars 0g, fibre 7g, protein 11g, salt 1.01g

Moroccan roasted vegetable soup

Roasted roots are great for making soup - try this one with parsnips, butternut squash and carrots.

 PREP 15 mins COOK 40 mins 4-5

- 1 red onion, cut into 8 wedges
- 300g/11oz each carrots, parsnips and peeled butternut squash, all cut into 2cm/¾in chunks
- 1 small potato, cut into 2cm/¾in chunks
- 2 garlic cloves
- 1 tbsp ras el hanout
- 1½ tbsp olive oil
- 1.3 litres/2¼ pints hot vegetable stock
- 6 tbsp Greek-style yogurt and 1 tbsp finely chopped mint, to serve (optional)

1 Heat oven to 200C/180C fan/gas 6. Tip all the vegetables and the garlic into a roasting tin. Sprinkle over the ras el hanout and some seasoning, drizzle over the oil and give everything a good stir. Roast for 30-35 mins, turning the vegetables over halfway, until they're tender and starting to caramelise a little.

2 Transfer the roasted veg to a large saucepan, pour over the hot stock and simmer for 5 mins. Purée the soup in a food processor, or in the pan with a stick blender, until smooth, then ladle into a flask for work. If eating at home, serve with a dollop of yogurt, a scattering of mint and a grinding of black pepper.

PER SERVING (4) 187 kcals, fat 6g, saturates 1g, carbs 29g, sugars 17g, fibre 10g, protein 5g, salt 0.9g

Chipotle black bean soup with lime-pickled onions

. . . .

The lime-pickled onions add a zingy flavour to this great Mexican-inspired low-fat and low-calorie soup.

 PREP 40 mins COOK 25 mins 2

- juice 2 limes
- 2 small red onions, thinly sliced
- ½ tbsp olive oil
- 2 garlic cloves, finely chopped
- ½ tbsp ground cumin
- ½ tbsp smoked paprika
- ½ tbsp chipotle paste or Tabasco, to taste
- 400g can black beans, drained and rinsed
- 400ml/14fl oz vegetable stock
- half-fat soured cream, coriander leaves and crisp tortillas, to serve

1 To make the lime-pickled onions, combine half the lime juice and half the onion in a small bowl, and season. Leave to pickle for 30 mins.

2 Meanwhile, heat the olive oil in a saucepan over a medium-high heat. Add the garlic and remaining onion, and season. Cook for 8 mins or until the onion is translucent. Add the spices and chipotle paste, cook for 1 min, then add the beans, stock and remaining lime juice. Simmer for 15 mins, then purée in a blender.

3 Pour the soup into a clean pan to reheat. Serve with a little of the drained pickled onions, topped with a small drizzle of soured cream and some coriander, and the tortillas on the side.

. . . .

PER SERVING 190 kcals, fat 5g, saturates 1g, carbs 26g, sugars 6g, fibre 10g, protein 9g, salt 0.8g

Carrot & tomato soup

This sweet and tangy soup is a family crowd pleaser. Serve with crusty bread if you aren't watching the calories!

 PREP 15 mins COOK 1 hr 15 mins 8

- 3 tbsp olive oil
- 2 onions, chopped
- 2 celery sticks, chopped
- 1.25kg/2lb 12oz carrots, sliced
- 250g/9oz floury potatoes, diced
- 5 bay leaves (fresh or dried)
- 500g carton passata
- 750g/1lb 10oz cherry tomatoes
- 2 vegetable stock cubes
- 1 tbsp sugar (caster or granulated)
- 1 tbsp red wine vinegar
- 250ml/9fl oz full-fat milk

1 Put the oil, onion and celery in your largest saucepan and cook gently until softened. Add the carrot and potato for a few mins, then add all the remaining ingredients, apart from the milk, with 1 litre/1¾ pints water. Bring to a simmer. Cover and simmer for 30 mins, then uncover and simmer for 20-30 mins.

2 Fish out the bay leaves and whizz the soup with a stick blender. Add the milk and as much water as you need. Season to taste, warm through and serve with a grinding of black pepper and crusty bread. Can be made and chilled up to 2 days ahead – or freeze for 1 month, then reheat gently.

PER SERVING 175 kcals, fat 7g, saturates 2g, carbs 24g, sugar 18g, fibre 8g, protein 5g, salt 1.0g

Moroccan chickpea soup

This super healthy soup is quick and easy to prepare. It will be on the table in under 30 mins and the chickpeas will leave you feeling satisfied for longer.

PREP 5 mins COOK 20 mins 4

- 1 tbsp olive oil
- 1 medium onion, chopped
- 2 sticks celery, chopped
- 2 tsp ground cumin
- 600ml/1 pint hot vegetable stock
- 400g can chopped plum tomatoes with garlic
- 400g can chickpeas, rinsed and drained
- 100g/4oz frozen broad beans
- zest and juice ½ lemon
- large handful coriander or parsley and flatbread, to serve

1 Heat the oil in a large saucepan, then fry the onion and celery gently for 10 mins until softened, stirring frequently. Tip in the cumin and fry for another min.

2 Turn up the heat, then add the stock, tomatoes and chickpeas, plus a good grind of black pepper. Simmer for 8 mins. Throw in the broad beans and lemon juice, cook for a further 2 mins. Season to taste, then top with a sprinkling of lemon zest and chopped herbs. Serve with flatbread.

PER SERVING 148 kcals, fat 5g, saturates 1g, carbs 17g, sugars 0g, fibre 6g, protein 9g, salt 1.07g

Carrot & coriander soup

. . . .

This simple, great-value soup uses just a few low-cost ingredients and is full of flavour.

PREP 15 mins COOK 30 mins 4

- 1 tbsp vegetable oil
- 1 onion, chopped
- 1 tsp ground coriander
- 1 potato, chopped
- 450g/1lb carrots, peeled and chopped
- 1.2 litres/2 pints vegetable or chicken stock
- handful coriander (about ½ a supermarket pack)

1 Heat the oil in a large pan, add the onion, then fry for 5 mins until softened. Stir in the ground coriander and potato, then cook for 1 min. Add the carrot and stock, bring to the boil, then reduce the heat. Cover and cook for 20 mins until the carrot is tender.

2 Tip into a food processor with the coriander, then blitz until smooth (you may need to do this in 2 batches). Return to the pan, taste, add salt if necessary, then reheat to serve.

. . . .

PER SERVING 115 kcals, fat 4g, saturates 1g, carbs 19g, sugars 12g, fibre 5g, protein 3g, salt 0.46g

Leek, bacon & potato soup

This soup will keep in the fridge for a couple of days. If you want to freeze it, add the cream after you reheat it.

PREP 30 mins COOK 30 mins   4

- 25g/1oz butter
- 3 rashers rindless streaky bacon, chopped
- 1 onion, chopped
- 400g pack trimmed leeks, sliced and well washed
- 3 medium potatoes, peeled and diced
- 1.4 litres/2½ pints hot vegetable stock
- 142ml pot single cream
- 4 rashers crisp streaky bacon, to serve

1 Melt the butter in a large pan, then fry the bacon and onion, stirring until they start to turn golden. Tip in the leek and potato, stir well, then cover and turn down the heat. Cook gently for 5 mins, shaking the pan every now and then to make sure that the mixture doesn't catch.

2 Pour in the stock, season well and bring to the boil. Cover and simmer for 20 mins until the vegetables are soft. Leave to cool for a few mins, then blend in a food processor in batches until smooth. Return to the pan, pour in the cream and stir well. Taste and season if necessary. Serve scattered with tasty crisp bacon and eat with toasted or warm crusty bread on the side.

PER SERVING 175 kcals, fat 11g, saturates 6g, carbs 15g, sugars 5g, fibre 4g, protein 6g, salt 0.68g

Watercress & artichoke soup

Potato gives this soup a thicker texture and adds valuable fibre.

 PREP 5 mins COOK 10 mins 2

- 100g/4oz potato, grated skin and all
- 8 spring onions, chopped
- 500ml/18fl oz low-sodium vegetable (or chicken) stock
- 2 x 85g bags watercress, a few sprigs reserved
- 150ml/¼ pint buttermilk
- 5 canned artichoke hearts, rinsed to remove excess salt, 1 chopped

1 Put the potato and spring onion in a pan and pour over the stock. Cover and cook for about 5 mins until the potato is tender.
2 Add the watercress, stir until wilted, then blitz with a stick blender or in a food processor until completely smooth. Add the buttermilk and the 4 whole artichokes and blitz again. Top with the chopped artichoke and watercress sprigs just before eating.

PER SERVING 214 kcals, fat 10g, saturates 2g, carbs 17g, sugars 8g, fibre 8g, protein 9g, salt 2.3g

Versatile veg soup

This basic soup recipe can be easily adapted to whatever veg you have to hand.

PREP 10 mins COOK 15 mins 2

- 200g/7oz chopped raw vegetables, such as onion, celery and carrot
- 300g/11oz potatoes, peeled and chopped
- 1 tbsp oil
- 700ml/1¼ pints stock
- crème fraîche and fresh herbs, to serve

1 Fry the chopped raw vegetables with the potato in the oil for a few mins until beginning to soften.
2 Cover with the stock and simmer for about 10-15 mins until the veg is tender. Blend until smooth, then season. Serve with a dollop of crème fraîche and some fresh herbs. Will freeze for up to 1 month.

PER SERVING 108 kcals, fat 1g, saturates 1g, fibre 4g, carbs 17g, sugars 1.6g, protein 8g, salt 0.84g

Thai pumpkin soup

Pumpkins are full of flavour and add something really special to this soup. It makes an impressive dinner party starter, which you can make ahead and reheat to serve.

🕐 PREP 25 mins COOK 40 mins 🥧 6

- 1.5kg/3lb 5oz pumpkin or squash, peeled and roughly chopped
- 4 tsp sunflower oil
- 1 onion, sliced
- 1 tbsp grated ginger
- 1 lemongrass stalk, bashed a little
- 3-4 tbsp Thai red curry paste
- 400ml can coconut milk
- 850ml/1½ pints vegetable stock
- lime juice and sugar, for seasoning
- 1 red chilli, sliced, to serve (optional)

1 Heat oven to 200C/180C fan/gas 6. Toss the pumpkin or squash in a roasting tin with half the oil and seasoning, then roast for 30 mins until golden and tender.
2 Meanwhile, put the remaining oil in a pan with the onion, ginger and lemongrass. Gently cook for 8-10 mins until softened. Stir in the curry paste for 1 min, followed by the roasted pumpkin, all but 3 tbsp of the coconut milk and the stock. Bring to a simmer, cook for 5 mins, then fish out the lemongrass.
3 Cool for a few mins, then whizz until smooth with a stick blender, or in a large blender in batches. Return to the pan to heat through, seasoning with salt, pepper, lime juice and sugar, if it needs it. Serve drizzled with the remaining coconut milk and scattered with chilli, if you like.

PER SERVING 192 kcals, fat 15g, saturates 10g, carbs 11g, sugars 9g, fibre 4g, protein 4g, salt 0.94g

Indian chickpea & vegetable soup

High in fibre, this soup counts as 2 of 5-a-day and packs a punch when it comes to flavour. Great as a take-to-work lunch.

PREP 10 mins COOK 15 mins 4

- 1 tbsp vegetable oil
- 1 large onion, chopped
- 1 tsp finely grated fresh root ginger
- 1 garlic clove, chopped
- 1 tbsp garam masala
- 850ml/1½ pints vegetable stock
- 2 large carrots, quartered lengthways and chopped
- 400g/14oz can chickpeas, drained
- 100g/4oz green beans, chopped

1 Heat the oil in a medium saucepan, then add the onion, ginger and garlic. Fry for 2 mins, then add the garam masala, give it 1 min more, then add the stock and carrots. Simmer for 10 mins, then add the chickpeas. Use a stick blender to whizz the soup a little.

2 Stir in the beans and simmer for 3 mins. Pack into a flask or, if you've got a microwave at work, chill and heat up for lunch. Great with naan bread.

PER SERVING 168 kcals, fat 6g, saturates 0g, carbs 23g, sugars 10g, fibre 6g, protein 7g, salt 0.66g

Miso chicken & rice soup

If you're watching your salt intake, use one of the low-salt soy sauces available. This soup is low fat and low calorie, perfect if you are following a low-fat or low-cal diet.

PREP 10 mins COOK 25 mins 2

- 500ml/18fl oz chicken stock
- 2 skinless chicken breasts
- 50g/2oz long-grain rice
- 8 Chantenay carrots, halved lengthways
- 2 tbsp miso paste
- 1 tbsp soy sauce
- 1 tbsp mirin
- 2 spring onions, sliced

1 Bring the stock to a gentle boil in a medium saucepan. Add the chicken breasts and simmer for 8 mins until cooked through. Remove from the pan and shred the meat.
2 Add the rice and carrots to the hot stock. Bring back up to the boil, cover with a lid, then reduce the heat and cook for 10 mins until the rice is cooked and the carrots are just tender.
3 Return the chicken to the pan and add the miso, soy and mirin. Scatter over the spring onions just before serving.

PER SERVING 274 kcals, fat 2g, saturates 1g, carbs 21g, sugars 10g, fibre 4g, protein 40g, salt 3.1g

Sherried squash soup

A great dinner party starter, this soup is a good source of vitamin C and counts as 2 of your 5-a-day.

PREP 20 mins COOK 30 mins 4

- 1 large onion, halved and sliced
- 2 tbsp olive oil
- 4 tbsp fino (dry) sherry
- 1kg/2lb 4oz butternut squash, peeled, deseeded and chopped
- 600ml/1 pint hot vegetable stock
- seed-bread croutons and flat-leaf parsley sprigs, to serve (optional)

1 Fry the onion in the oil for 5 mins until softened. Add the sherry and squash and sizzle for 1-2 mins. Pour in the stock, then cover and simmer for 20 mins until the squash is tender when pierced with a knife.

2 Whizz in a food processor until smooth. Will keep in the fridge for 2 days, or freeze for 6 weeks. When ready to eat, reheat until bubbling and serve in small portions topped with seed-bread croutons and a parsley sprig.

PER SERVING 183 kcals, fat 6g, saturates 1g, carbs 26g, sugar 15g, protein 4g, fibre 5g, salt 0.22g

Chunky Mediterranean fish soup

Hoki is a New Zealand import available in the freezer section in supermarkets. It's a relative of cod and has a firm, white-textured flesh. You could also use cod.

PREP 5 mins COOK 8-10 mins 4

- 500g tub Napoletana pasta sauce
- 450ml/16fl oz fish stock
- 2 courgettes, finely sliced
- 1 bulb fennel, finely sliced
- 450g/1lb hoki fillets, defrosted
- handful basil leaves, torn
- 1 tsp chipotle chillies in adobo sauce or chilli paste, to serve
- 5 tbsp half-fat crème fraîche, to serve

1 Put the pasta sauce and stock into a large saucepan, bring to the boil and simmer for 2-3 mins. Add the courgettes and fennel and simmer for 2 mins.
2 Cut the hoki fillets into 4cm/1½in pieces. Add to the soup and poach over a low heat for about 2-3 mins or until the fish is cooked through. Don't stir too often or the fish will break up. Gently stir in the basil and adjust the seasoning.
3 Mix the chipotle chilli mix or chilli paste with the crème fraîche and season. Ladle the soup into bowls and spoon a dollop of crème fraîche on top.

PER SERVING 164 kcals, fat 4g, saturates 1g, carbs 9g, sugars 5g, fibre 3g, protein 23g, salt 1.83g

Creamy fish & mussel soup

Using only 5 ingredients, on the table in under 30 mins, this Med-style supper is perfect if you fancy something a little special with minimal effort!

PREP 10 mins COOK 20 mins 4

- 500g pack mussels in creamy sauce
- 1 litre/1¾ pints strong, hot fish stock
- 500g/1lb 2oz floury potatoes, cut into sugarcube-sized pieces
- 200g/8oz mixed fish
- small bunch flat-leaf parsley

1 Drain the sauce from the mussels into a large saucepan and add the stock. Tip in the potatoes, cover and bring to the boil. Once boiling, take off the lid and simmer for about 12 mins or until the potatoes are very tender.

2 Meanwhile, cut the fish into large chunks and roughly chop the parsley. Stir the fish and mussels into the soup, then bring back to a simmer for about 3 mins or until the fish has changed colour and flakes easily. Stir in most of the parsley, then serve scattered with the rest of the parsley and eat with crusty bread.

PER SERVING 185 kcals, fat 7g, saturates 3g, carbs 8g, sugars 1g, fibre 1g, protein 22g, salt 3.45g

Thai chicken & mushroom broth

Serve with extra lime juice, sugar and fish sauce on the side so everyone can adjust their own bowlfuls.

 PREP 10 mins COOK 10 mins 4

- 1 litre/1¾ pints hot chicken stock
- 1 tbsp Thai red curry paste
- 1 tbsp Thai fish sauce
- 2 tsp sugar
- zest and juice 2 limes
- 100g/4oz Portobello mushrooms, sliced
- bunch spring onions, sliced, whites and greens separated
- 200g/7oz leftover chicken, shredded

1 Tip the stock into a saucepan, then stir in the curry paste, fish sauce, sugar, lime juice and most of the zest. Bring to the boil, then add the mushrooms and whites of the spring onion. Cover, then simmer for 2 mins.

2 Stir in the chicken and most of the spring onion greens to gently heat through, then serve ladled into bowls and scattered with the remaining lime zest.

PER SERVING 179 kcals, fat 6g, saturates 1g, carbs 6g, sugar 4g, fibre 1g, protein 25g, salt 2.32g

Oriental pork balls in hoisin broth

Satisfying and filling, make this hearty recipe when you fancy a delicious quick-and-easy meal.

PREP 20 mins COOK 10 mins 4

- 500g pack lean pork mince
- 2 tbsp soy sauce
- 2 tbsp cornflour
- 1 tsp Chinese five-spice powder
- 225g can water chestnuts, drained, half finely chopped, half sliced
- 500ml/18fl oz chicken stock
- 3 tbsp hoisin sauce
- thumb-sized piece ginger, shredded
- 2 large carrots, shaved into strips with a potato peeler
- 8 Chinese leaves, thick part sliced, leaves shredded
- 300g pack beansprouts
- bunch spring onions, cut into lengths, plus a few tops chopped, to serve

1 Tip the mince into a bowl with the soy, cornflour, five-spice, chopped water chestnuts and some black pepper. Work everything together, then shape into 12 meatballs.

2 Pour the stock into a wide, deep pan and stir in the hoisin and ginger. Add the meatballs, then cover and poach for 5 mins. Drop in the carrot, Chinese leaves, beansprouts, spring onion and sliced chestnuts, then put on the lid and simmer for 5 mins. Ladle into bowls, then serve scattered with spring onion tops.

PER SERVING 366 kcals, fat 14g, saturates 5g, carbs 29g, sugars 11g, fibre 4g, protein 32g, salt 2.5g

Prawn & fennel bisque

The prawn shells give a deep seafood flavour to this luxurious soup. It's quite a rich dish, so feels indulgent without the calories.

PREP 30 mins COOK 55 mins 8

- 450g/1lb raw tiger prawns in their shells
- 4 tbsp olive oil
- 1 large onion, chopped
- 1 large fennel bulb, chopped, fronds reserved
- 2 carrots, chopped
- 150ml/¼ pint dry white wine
- 1 tbsp brandy
- 400g can chopped tomatoes
- 1 litre/1¾ pints fish stock
- 2 generous pinches paprika

TO SERVE
- 150ml pot double cream
- 8 tiger prawns, shelled but tail tips left on (optional)
- fennel fronds (optional)

1 Shell the prawns, then fry the shells in the oil in a large pan for about 5 mins. Add the onion, fennel and carrot and cook for about 10 mins until the veg start to soften. Pour in the wine and brandy, bubble hard for about 1 min, then add the tomatoes, stock and paprika. Cover and simmer for 30 mins. Meanwhile, chop the prawns.

2 Blitz the soup with a stick blender or food processor, then press the soup through a sieve into a bowl.

3 Tip back into a clean pan, add the prawns and cook for 10 mins, then blitz again until smooth. You can make and chill this a day ahead or freeze it for 1 month. Thaw overnight in the fridge.

4 To serve, gently reheat in a pan with the cream. If garnishing, cook the 8 prawns in a little butter. Spoon the soup into the bowls and top with the prawns and snipped fennel fronds.

PER SERVING 120 kcals, fat 6g, saturates 1g, carbs 7g, sugars 6g, fibre 3g, protein 7g, salt 1.17g

Moroccan harira

This vegetarian version of the classic Moroccan soup contains turmeric, which is good for heart and brain health and inflammatory conditions like arthritis.

🕐 PREP 15 mins COOK 50 mins   4

- 1-2 tbsp rapeseed oil
- 2 large onions, finely chopped
- 4 garlic cloves, chopped
- 2 tsp turmeric
- 2 tsp cumin
- ½ tsp cinnamon
- 2 red chillies, deseeded and sliced
- 500g carton passata
- 1.7 litres/3 pints low-sodium vegetable bouillon
- 175g/6oz dried green lentils
- 2 carrots, chopped into pieces
- 1 sweet potato, peeled and diced
- 5 celery sticks, chopped into small pieces
- ⅔ small pack coriander, few sprigs reserved, the rest chopped
- 1 lemon, cut into 4 wedges, to serve

1 Heat the oil in a large non-stick sauté pan over a medium heat and fry the onion and garlic until starting to soften. Tip in the spices and chilli, stir briefly, then pour in the passata and stock. Add the lentils, carrot, sweet potato and celery, and bring to the boil.

2 Cover the pan and leave to simmer for about 30 mins, then cook uncovered for a further 5-10 mins until the vegetables and lentils are tender. Stir in the chopped coriander and serve in bowls with lemon wedges for squeezing over, and the reserved coriander sprinkled over.

PER SERVING 335 kcals, fat 6g, saturates 1g, carbs 48g, sugars 21g, fibre 13g, protein 16g, salt 0.2g

Salmon with miso vegetables

After a busy day, this is so quick to prepare you won't be tempted to snack while you wait for it to cook.

 PREP 5 mins COOK 10 mins 2

- 18g pack instant miso soup
- 2 garlic cloves, finely grated
- 1 tbsp rice vinegar or white wine vinegar
- 100g/4oz thin-stemmed broccoli, cut into lengths and small florets
- 4 spring onions, chopped
- 100g/4oz beansprouts
- 2 big handfuls watercress (about 50-85g/2-3oz)
- 240g pack of 2 skinless salmon fillets

1 Make up the soup mix in a large pan with 500ml/18fl oz water and bring to the boil with the garlic and vinegar. Add the broccoli and spring onions, cover and cook for 5 mins.
2 Stir in the beansprouts and watercress, top with the salmon and cover again. Cook for 4 mins until the salmon flakes easily. Serve in bowls with a fork and spoon.

PER SERVING 282 kcals, fat 15g, saturates 3g, carbs 6g, sugars 4g, fibre 5g, protein 31g, salt 1.2g

Tom yum (hot & sour) soup with prawns

This hot and sour soup is one of the best-known Thai dishes and delivers an incredible punch with just a few ingredients.

 PREP 15 mins COOK 8 mins 2

- 700ml/1½ pints chicken stock
- 1 lemongrass stalk, bruised and cut into large pieces
- 5 thick slices galangal
- 3 coriander roots or 6 stems, bruised, plus leaves to garnish
- 3 lime leaves, torn
- 6 large prawns, shelled
- 3 tbsp Thai fish sauce
- 6 small green chillies, chopped
- 4 tbsp lime juice

1 Bring the stock to a boil in a medium-sized saucepan. Add the lemongrass, galangal, coriander roots and lime leaves, then simmer for 2 mins.

2 Add the prawns, fish sauce, chillies and lime juice, then return to the boil. Taste and adjust the seasoning with either more lime juice or fish sauce, then garnish with coriander leaves and serve.

PER SERVING 90 kcals, fat 1g, saturates 0g, carbs 5g, sugars 1g, fibre 2g, protein 17g, salt 5.8g

Beetroot soup with feta, radish & croutons

. . . .

Serve this low-fat soup hot or cold. It's light, refreshing and the beetroot gives it a wonderful earthy flavour.

PREP 20 mins plus chilling (optional) COOK 55 mins 4

- 2 tbsp olive oil
- 1 large onion, finely chopped
- 2 garlic cloves, crushed
- 1kg/2lb 4oz fresh beetroot, peeled and diced (wear rubber gloves to stop your hands turning pink)
- 1.5 litres/2¾ pints vegetable stock
- ½ small loaf sourdough, diced into large croutons
- 100g/4oz radishes, finely sliced
- 100g/4oz feta, crumbled

1 Heat 1 tbsp oil in a large saucepan and add the chopped onion, frying for 5 mins until slightly softened. Add the garlic, stirring to combine for 1 min, then toss in the beetroot and cook for 15 mins.

2 Pour in the stock and bring to the boil. Once boiling, reduce the heat and simmer uncovered for 30 mins or until the beetroot is tender. Season well and leave to cool a little before blending.

3 Meanwhile, heat the grill to high and put the sourdough croutons on a baking sheet drizzled with the remaining 1 tbsp oil and toast until golden. Whizz the soup until smooth using a stick blender.

4 If serving the soup chilled, leave to cool completely and chill for a couple of hours before serving. If serving hot, warm through in the pan for 2-3 mins. Serve in bowls or mugs with the croutons, radishes and crumbled feta scattered over.

. . . .

PER SERVING 403 kcals, fat 13g, saturates 4g, carbs 52g, sugars 25g, fibre 11g, protein 15g, salt 2.9g

Nettle soup

Once cooked, nettles have a mild spinach or cabbage flavour. Using dead nettles here saves your hands from being stung, and gives you lovely flowers to use as a garnish.

🕐 PREP 20 mins COOK 30 mins   🥧 4-6

- 1 tbsp olive oil, plus extra for drizzling
- 1 onion, chopped
- 1 carrot, diced
- 1 leek, washed and finely sliced
- 1 large floury potato (Maris Piper or similar), thinly sliced
- 1 litre/1¾ pints vegetable stock
- 400g/14oz stinging or dead nettles, washed, leaves picked
- 50g/2oz butter, diced
- 50ml/2fl oz double cream

1 Heat the oil in a large saucepan over a medium heat. Add the onion, carrot, leek and potato, and cook for 10 mins until the vegetables start to soften. Add the stock and cook for a further 10-15 mins until the potato is soft.
2 Add the nettle leaves, simmer for 1 min to wilt, then blend the soup. Season to taste, then stir in the butter and cream. Serve the soup drizzled with extra oil and scattered with dead nettle flowers, if you have them.

. . . .
PER SERVING 323 kcals, fat 21g, saturates 11g, carbs 21g, sugars 7g, fibre 9g, protein 6g, salt 0.9g

Fresh pea & lovage soup

Lovage has a celery-like flavour, but if you can't find it, substitute with mint. Serve this soup hot or chilled – cook the peas lightly so that they keep their sweet flavour.

PREP 20 mins plus cooling (optional) COOK 10 mins 8

- approx 2.5kg/5½lb fresh peas in their pods (or 900g/2lb podded or frozen), plus 16 whole pods to decorate
- 100g/4oz unsalted butter
- 175g/6oz spring onions
- 1 garlic clove, finely chopped
- 1.5 litres/2¾ pints vegetable stock
- 100g/4oz crème fraîche
- bunch lovage (about 10 sprigs), leaves picked (or use a small bunch mint)

1 Shell the peas, leaving 16 of the best-looking ones whole. Melt half the butter in a large pan, then gently cook the spring onion and garlic with the lid on for 5 mins, without colouring. Add the stock, bring to the boil, then add the peas and whole pods and simmer for 2-3 mins until tender.

2 Fish out the whole pods and refresh under cold water. Tip in the crème fraîche, then the lovage or mint, and blitz with a stick blender until smooth. Season to taste. Leave to cool, then chill in the fridge if serving cold.

3 If you're eating the soup hot, bring to a gentle simmer but don't boil. To serve, ladle into bowls, decorate each with 2 whole, split pea pods and serve with a stack of toasted bread on the side.

PER SERVING 251 kcals, fat 17g, saturates 10g, carbs 16g, sugars 5g, fibre 7g, protein 9g, salt 0.25g

Summer vegetable minestrone

This soup is packed with goodness, providing 3 of your 5-a-day. It's a lighter, greener version of the wintery classic.

 PREP 10 mins COOK 30 mins 4

- 3 tbsp olive oil
- 2 leeks, finely sliced
- 2 celery sticks, finely chopped
- 2 courgettes, quartered lengthways, then sliced
- 4 garlic cloves, finely chopped
- 1 litre/1¾ pints vegetable stock
- 250g/9oz asparagus, woody ends removed, chopped
- 100g/4oz peas, fresh or frozen
- 200g/7oz broad beans, double-podded if you have time
- small bunch basil, most chopped

1 Heat the oil in a large saucepan, add the leek and celery, and cook for 8 mins until soft. Add the courgette and garlic. Cook gently for 5 mins more.
2 Pour in the stock and simmer, covered, for 10 mins. Add the asparagus, peas and broad beans, and cook for a further 4 mins, until just cooked through. Stir in the chopped basil and season well. Scatter with basil leaves and serve with crusty bread.

PER SERVING 188 kcals, fat 11g, saturates 2g, carbs 13g, sugars 7g, fibre 11g, protein 10g, salt 0.7g

Pea & mint soup with crisp prosciutto strips

Crisp prosciutto strips add a savoury, yet lean hit of flavour, making this low-fat, low-calorie soup all the more delicious.

 PREP 5 mins COOK 15 mins 2

- 2 leeks, well washed and thinly sliced
- 200g/7oz potato (unpeeled), scrubbed and grated
- 500ml/18fl oz chicken or vegetable stock
- 200g/7oz frozen peas
- 150g pot 0% bio yogurt
- 2 tbsp chopped mint, plus extra to serve
- 2 slices prosciutto, all excess fat removed

1 Put the leeks, potato and stock in a pan and bring to the boil. Cover and simmer for 8 mins.

2 Tip in the peas, cover and cook for 5 mins more. Take off the heat and blitz with a stick blender (or in a food processor) until smooth, then stir in the yogurt and mint.

3 Meanwhile, lay the slices of prosciutto in a large non-stick frying pan in a single layer and heat until crisp. Allow to cool a little, then tear into strips, ready to sprinkle over the soup with some ground black pepper and mint. Will keep in the fridge for 2 days.

PER SERVING 276 kcals, fat 5g, saturates 2g, carbs 38g, sugars 14g, fibre 14g, protein 20g, salt 1.9g

Summery soup with pesto

. . . .

Super healthy, low fat and quick to throw together – this soup is the perfect go-to dish if you've friends coming over last minute.

 PREP 15 mins NO COOK 4

- 1 courgette, halved and thinly sliced
- 200g/7oz fresh or frozen peas, defrosted
- 1 vegetable stock cube
- 250g bag ready-cooked basmati rice
- 100g bag baby spinach
- 4 tbsp vegetarian pesto
- olive oil (optional), for drizzling
- grated cheese, to serve

1 Boil the kettle. Tip the courgette and peas into a large bowl, then cover with boiling water. Cover the bowl, then leave for 3 mins until the vegetables have softened slightly. Meanwhile, re-boil the kettle and make up 600ml/1 pint of stock, then taste it for seasoning as this is the base of the soup.

2 Drain the veg, then put back into the bowl along with the rice and spinach. Pour over the hot stock, then cover and leave for another 2 mins until heated through and the spinach has wilted.

3 Season to taste, then ladle the soup into serving bowls. Add a swirl of pesto, olive oil, if using, and the grated cheese. Serve with some crusty bread.

. . . .

PER SERVING 176 kcals, fat 5g, saturates 2g, carbs 25g, sugars 0g, fibre 4g, protein 9g, salt 1g

Chilled pea & watercress soup

A great starter idea for a summer lunch or dinner. The soup can be made ahead and left in the fridge to chill, so you can spend more time with your guests.

 PREP 5-10 mins NO COOK 4

- 454g pack frozen peas
- 85g bag watercress, roughly torn
- 850ml/1½ pints vegetable stock
- juice and zest of 1 small lemon
- 3 tbsp natural yogurt
- ice cubes, to serve

1 Place all of the ingredients, except the yogurt and ice cubes, in a blender. Don't overfill your machine – you may need to do this in 2 batches. Whizz everything for a couple of minutes until smooth and speckled with the watercress.

2 Season if you want to, then serve straight away or chill until needed. The soup will keep in the fridge in an airtight container for up to a 2 days (give it a good stir before serving) or can be frozen for up to 1 month.

3 Serve the soup drizzled with the yogurt and a couple of ice cubes to make it even more refreshing.

PER SERVING 86 kcals, fat 1g, saturates 1g, carbs 11g, sugars 0g, fibre 6g, protein 8g, salt 0.73g

Spicy pepper & tomato soup with cucumber yogurt

Delicious hot or cold, this low-fat, Med-style soup is perfect as a cooling lunch on a hot summer's day. Packed with veg, it's 3 of your 5-a-day.

PREP 15 mins COOK 30 mins 4

- 2 tbsp olive oil, plus extra to serve
- 2 onions, finely sliced
- 1 carrot, finely chopped
- 3 red peppers, roughly chopped
- 3 garlic cloves, sliced
- 1 red chilli, sliced
- 400g can chopped tomatoes
- 850ml-1 litre/1½-1¾ pints vegetable stock or bouillon
- 4 tbsp Greek-style yogurt
- ½ cucumber, halved, deseeded, coarsely grated and squeezed of excess water
- few mint leaves, chopped

1 Heat the oil in a large saucepan. Tip in the onion, carrot and pepper. Cook gently for 15 mins, to soften. Add the garlic and chilli, and cook for a few mins more. Pour over the chopped tomatoes and 800ml/1 pint 9fl oz of the stock. Bring to the boil and simmer for 10-15 mins until the veg is completely tender.

2 Meanwhile, mix the yogurt, cucumber and mint in a bowl, and season.

3 Blitz the soup with a stick blender until smooth, using the extra stock to thin if it has become too thick. Heat through, season and spoon into bowls. Serve with a dollop of the yogurt mixture on top and a drizzle of olive oil.

PER SERVING 221 kcals, fat 11g, saturates 4g, carbs 22g, sugars 19g, fibre 7g, protein 7g, salt 0.8g

Green gazpacho

This chilled soup is deceptively easy to prepare and will wow your guests at a spring or summer garden party. Adding the flower ice cubes adds a professional finish.

PREP 15 mins plus chilling NO COOK 4

- edible petals and flowers, such as viola, rose, borage, nasturtium and pansy
- 100g bag baby spinach
- 2 garlic cloves
- 1 large cucumber, deseeded and chopped
- ½ green chilli, deseeded
- ½ small pack each parsley, basil and mint
- 1 ripe avocado, stoned and peeled
- 4 spring onions, trimmed
- 200g/7oz natural yogurt
- 2 tbsp Sherry vinegar
- drizzle of extra virgin olive oil or rapeseed oil, to serve
- handful pea shoots, to serve

1 To make this soup extra special, freeze the edible petals and flowers into ice cubes. These will keep for up to 2 months in the freezer.
2 Put all the ingredients, except the oil and pea shoots, into a food processor with a good pinch of salt and black pepper and blitz, adding enough water to get a soupy consistency. Taste, and add a little more vinegar and seasoning if necessary. Chill for up to 24 hours, or at least 2 hours.
3 To serve, divide into shallow soup bowls, float a few ice cubes in each bowl and add a scattering of pea shoots and a drizzle of oil before serving.

PER SERVING 120 kcals, fat 8g, saturates 2g, carbs 7g, sugars 6g, fibre 3g, protein 6g, salt 0.3g

Kale & apple soup with walnuts

This fibre-packed vegetarian soup is given added depth by adding a sweet apple and crunchy walnut topping.

 PREP 20 mins COOK 15 mins 2

- 8 walnut halves, broken into pieces
- 1 onion, finely chopped
- 2 carrots, coarsely grated
- 2 red apples, unpeeled and finely chopped
- 1 tbsp cider vinegar
- 500ml/18fl oz low-sodium vegetable stock
- 200g/7oz kale, roughly chopped
- 20g pack of dried apple crisps (optional)

1 In a dry, non-stick frying pan, cook the walnut pieces for 2-3 mins until toasted, turning frequently so they don't burn. Take off the heat and allow to cool.

2 Put the onion, carrot, apple, vinegar and stock in a large saucepan and bring to the boil. Reduce the heat and simmer for 10 mins, stirring occasionally.

3 Once the onion is translucent and the apples start to soften, add the kale and simmer for an additional 2 mins. Carefully transfer to a blender and blend until very smooth. Pour into bowls and serve topped with the toasted walnuts and a sprinkling of apple crisps, if you like.

PER SERVING 403 kcals, fat 21g, saturates 2g, carbs 36g, sugars 25g, fibre 9g, protein 12g, salt 0.8g

Quick gazpacho

This chilled soup is perfect on a hot summer's day. It's an excellent source of vitamin C and will be on the table in 10 mins, so it's sure to be one of your weeknight staples.

 PREP 10 mins NO COOK 1

- 250ml/9fl oz passata
- 1 red pepper, deseeded and chopped
- 1 red chilli, deseeded and chopped
- 1 garlic clove, crushed
- 1 tsp sherry vinegar
- juice ½ lime
- ice cubes, to serve

1 In a blender (or with a stick blender), whizz together the passata, red pepper, chilli, garlic, sherry vinegar and lime juice until smooth. Season to taste, then serve with ice cubes.

PER SERVING 126 kcals, fat 1g, saturates 0g, fibre 3g, carbs 26g, sugars 18g, protein 5g, salt 1.26g

Salmorejo (rustic tomato soup with olive oil & bread)

· ·

This deep-flavoured soup originates from southern Spain and is served cold. Spiked with cumin and Sherry vinegar, it is a great way to use up late-summer tomatoes.

🕐 PREP 25 mins plus 2 hrs chilling COOK 5 mins   4

- 1 tsp cumin seeds
- 200g/7oz sourdough bread, crusts removed, torn into chunks
- 1kg/2lb 4oz very ripe tomatoes
- 2 fat garlic cloves
- 2 flame-roasted red peppers, peeled and deseeded (from a jar is fine)
- 1 tbsp Sherry vinegar, to taste

TO SERVE

- 2 hard-boiled eggs, roughly chopped
- 4 slices Serrano ham, roughly chopped
- small handful parsley, roughly chopped
- drizzle of extra virgin olive oil

1 Put a frying pan on a low heat, add the cumin seeds and toast for 1-2 mins, stirring frequently. Crush the seeds using a pestle and mortar. Soak the bread in water for 10 mins.

2 Meanwhile, to skin the tomatoes, cut a cross in the skin on the top and bottom of each tomato, then put them in a bowl and cover with boiling water. After 1-2 mins, drain the tomatoes and plunge into a bowl of ice-cold water. The skins should now peel off easily.

3 Cut the flesh into quarters and remove the seeds and pulp. Put the seeds and pulp in a sieve over a bowl and squish to release all the juices from around the seeds. Keep the juice and discard the seeds and pulp.

4 Put the garlic, tomatoes and juice, peppers and cumin in a food processor or blender. Squeeze the water from the bread, then add. Season and blitz until very smooth. Add the vinegar, cover and chill for at least 2 hours.

5 Serve the soup in bowls with the toppings.

· ·
PER SERVING 204 kcals, fat 2g, saturates 1g, carbs 36g, sugars 9g, fibre 5g, protein 8g, salt 0.7g

Egg drop chicken noodle soup

This low-fat soup requires minimal effort and is full of flavour. Use rice noodles if you prefer a more Asian twist, and swap Sherry vinegar for rice wine vinegar.

PREP 5 mins COOK 10 mins 4

- 2 skinless chicken breasts, diced
- 1.2 litres/2 pints low-sodium chicken stock
- 140g/5oz wholewheat noodles
- 140g/5oz baby corn, halved lengthways, or frozen sweetcorn
- 2 eggs, beaten
- squeeze lemon juice
- ½ tbsp Sherry vinegar
- 2 spring onions, finely chopped

1 Place the chicken and stock in a large pan and bring to a simmer for 5 mins. Meanwhile, cook the noodles following pack instructions.

2 Add the baby corn to the stock and cook for 2 mins. Stir the broth vigorously, then while it's still swirling, hold a fork over the pan. Pour the eggs over the prongs in a slow stream. Stir again in the same direction then turn off the heat. Add a squeeze of lemon juice and the vinegar.

3 Drain the noodles and divide into 4 bowls. Ladle over the egg drop broth, scatter with spring onions and serve.

PER SERVING 273 kcals, fat 6g, saturates 1g, carbs 30g, sugars 2g, fibre 3g, protein 26g, salt 1.04g

Coconut noodle & vegetable soup

Keep washing-up to a minimum with this low-fat, one-pan, Asian-style soup.

PREP 10 mins COOK 15 mins 4

- 1-2 tbsp Thai green curry paste
- 1 tsp groundnut oil
- 700ml/1¼ pints vegetable stock
- 300ml/½ pint reduced-fat coconut milk
- 200g/7oz thick rice noodles
- 200g/7oz chestnut mushrooms, sliced
- 140g/5oz sugar snap peas, halved
- 100g/4oz beansprouts
- 1½ tbsp Thai fish sauce
- juice 1 lime
- 3 spring onions, shredded, to serve
- a few mint and coriander leaves, to serve

1 Put a large pan over a medium heat. Cook the curry paste in the oil for 1 min until it starts to release its aroma. Pour in the stock and coconut milk and bring to the boil. Reduce the heat to a simmer and stir in the noodles. Simmer for 7 mins, then stir in the mushrooms and sugar snaps. Cook for 3 mins more, then add the beansprouts, fish sauce and lime juice. Remove the pan from the heat.

2 Ladle the noodles and soup into bowls, then scatter with the spring onion, mint and coriander to serve.

PER SERVING 296 kcals, fat 10g, saturates 7g, carbs 48g, sugars 5g, fibre 3g, protein 7g, salt 1.97g

Rocket & courgette soup with goat's cheese croutons

. . . .

This light soup is a good source of folic acid and vitamin C and counts as 2 of your 5-a-day.

 PREP: 15 mins COOK: 25 mins 4

- 1 onion, finely diced
- 1 tsp olive oil or knob of butter
- 1 medium potato, finely diced
- 4 courgettes, grated or chopped
- 100g/4oz rocket, roughly chopped
- 850ml/1½ pints vegetable stock
- 8 thin slices baguette
- 150g pack soft goat's cheese

1 Cook the onion gently in the olive oil or butter for 5-10 mins, until soft. Add the potato and cook for 5 mins, then add the courgette, rocket, stock and plenty of seasoning. Bring to a simmer and cook for 5 mins, until the courgette feels soft.

2 Whizz the soup in a blender, or use a stick blender, until smooth. Return to the pan and keep warm.

3 Toast the baguette slices, spread each with a little goat's cheese, then grill if you like, or serve as it is with the soup.

. . . .

PER SERVING 233 kcals, fat 9g, saturates 4g, carbs 28g, sugars 7g, fibre 4g, protein 12g, salt 1.36g

Summer pistou

This is a cross between a soup and a stew, packed with veg and flavoured with aromatic basil.

PREP 10 mins COOK 20 mins 4

- 1 tbsp rapeseed oil
- 2 leeks, finely sliced
- 1 large courgette, finely diced
- 1 litre/1¾ pints boiling vegetable stock (made with low-sodium bouillon)
- 400g can cannellini or haricot beans, drained
- 200g/7oz green beans, chopped
- 3 tomatoes, chopped
- 3 garlic cloves, finely chopped
- small pack basil
- 40g/1½oz freshly grated Parmesan

1 Heat the oil in a large pan and fry the leeks and courgette for 5 mins to soften. Pour in the stock, add three-quarters of the cannellini beans with the green beans, half the tomatoes, and simmer for 5-8 mins until the vegetables are tender.

2 Meanwhile, blitz the remaining beans and tomatoes, the garlic and basil in a food processor (or in a bowl with a stick blender) until smooth, then stir in the Parmesan. Stir the sauce into the soup, cook for 1 min, then ladle half into bowls or pour into a flask for a packed lunch. Chill the remainder. Will keep for a couple of days.

PER SERVING 209 kcals, fat 8g, saturates 3g, carbs 18g, sugars 6g, fibre 10g, protein 12g, salt 0.2g

Creamy chilled basil, pea & lettuce soup

A refreshing soup to serve as a starter or in shot glasses as a canapé.

PREP 10 mins plus chilling COOK 5 mins 4

- 300g/11oz fresh or frozen peas
- 1 large bunch basil, leaves only
- 1 head soft lettuce, core removed and shredded
- 850ml/1½ pints cold vegetable stock
- 200ml pot crème fraîche

1 Cook the peas in boiling water for 3 mins. Drain and cool with cold running water. Put the peas, basil, lettuce, vegetable stock and three-quarters of the crème fraîche together in a blender and process until smooth. Do this in 2 batches.

2 Season, cover and chill for at least 1 hour before serving. Add a swirl of remaining crème fraîche and serve.

PER SERVING 263 kcals, fat 21g, saturates 13g, carbs 11g, sugars 0g, fibre 4g, protein 8g, salt 1g

Steamed clams in saffron & spring green broth

This makes a smart, quick starter. The clams are as salty, so do use low-sodium stock and you won't need to add salt during cooking.

 PREP 5 mins COOK 10 mins 4 as a starter

- 700ml/1¼ pints hot low-sodium chicken stock
- 75g/3oz chorizo, diced
- 1 garlic clove, thinly sliced
- pinch of saffron strands
- 2 small heads spring greens, finely shredded
- 1kg/2lb 4oz small live clams or cockles, washed well
- 2 tbsp parsley, finely chopped
- 1 tbsp olive oil
- lemon wedges, to serve

1 Place the stock, chorizo, garlic and saffron in a large pan and bring to the boil. Add the greens, cover and cook for 2 mins until completely wilted.

2 Add the clams, cover and cook over a high heat for 4-5 mins until every clam has opened. Stir in the chopped parsley.

3 Using a slotted spoon, divide the greens and clams into large, shallow bowls then ladle over the broth. Drizzle with oil and serve with the lemon to squeeze over.

PER SERVING 156 kcals, fat 10g, saturates 2g, carbs 5g, sugars 3g, fibre 3g, protein 13g, salt 0.88g

Spring vegetable broth with shredded chicken

. . . .

Broth isn't just for winter. Try out this version with plenty of greens and top with parmesan toasts for added crunch.

PREP 40 mins plus standing COOK 20 mins 2

- 1 tbsp olive oil
- 1 large chicken breast, skin on
- 500ml/18fl oz chicken stock
- 1 slice sourdough bread, cut into cubes
- 2 tbsp grated Parmesan
- 2 large handfuls spring greens, finely sliced
- 4 asparagus spears, woody ends removed, halved and cut into chunky pieces
- 40g/1½oz fresh or frozen peas
- 400g can borlotti beans, drained and rinsed

1 Heat oven to 200C/180C fan/gas 6. Heat 1 tsp of the oil in a pan, brown the chicken, then remove. Bring the stock to the boil in the same pan, add the chicken and cook for 5 mins. Turn off the heat, cover with a lid and leave to stand for 30 mins.

2 Put the bread cubes on a baking tray. Drizzle with the remaining oil, some salt and the Parmesan. Bake for 6 mins until crunchy and golden. Remove and scrape off the tray onto a plate.

3 Remove the chicken from the pan and slice it. Bring the stock to the boil again and add the greens, asparagus and peas. Cook for 1 min, then add the beans and chicken. Heat everything through, then pour into bowls and top with the Parmesan toast to serve.

. . . .

PER SERVING 465 kcals, fat 17g, saturates 6g, carbs 28g, sugars 4g, fibre 12g, protein 43g, salt 1.2g

Cheat's chicken ramen

· ·

This low-fat, low-calorie ramen is a quick and satisfying crowd pleaser. Serve with extra soy sauce on the side if you like.

🕐 PREP 10 mins COOK 15-20 mins   🥧 4

- 1.2 litres/2 pints good-quality chicken stock
- small pack coriander, stalks and leaves separated
- 1 red chilli (deseeded if you don't like it too hot), sliced
- 2 tbsp light soy sauce
- 100g/4oz grey oyster mushrooms, sliced
- 100g pack baby pak choi
- 2 skinless cooked chicken breasts, sliced
- 100g/4oz egg noodles
- 50g/2oz sliced bamboo shoots

1 Set a large saucepan over a medium heat and pour in the stock. Finely chop the coriander stalks and add to the stock with most of the chilli. Bring to the boil and add 200ml/7fl oz water. Once boiled, reduce the heat and simmer for 5-10 mins to infuse the coriander and chilli.

2 Add the soy sauce and a grinding of black pepper, then the mushrooms, pak choi, chicken and noodles. Simmer for 2 mins until the noodles soften, before adding the bamboo shoots.

3 Serve in deep bowls topped with coriander leaves and the remaining chilli slices.

· ·

PER SERVING 255 kcals, fat 5g, saturates 2g, carbs 20g, sugars 2g, fibre 4g, protein 30g, salt 2.4g

Index